MASTERS MIND & BODY

Advanced Kung Fu techniques for personal transformation

Dr Matthew Mills

> "Man reinvents himself daily"
> Jean Paul Sartre

Masters Mind and Body
A Qi Publishing book

This book is published by Qi Publishing,
an imprint of
Continuo Creative Ltd
39-41 North Road
London N7 9DP

www.mindandbodymetamorphosis.co.uk

ISBN 978-0-9559271-0-2

Text, design, photography and illustration
Copyright © 2008 Dr Matthew Mills

All rights reserved. The right of Doctor Matthew Mills to be identified as the author of this work has been asserted in accordance with the Copyright, Designs and Patents Act of 1988

This book is protected by copyright. No part of this book may be reproduced, stored in a retrieval system, or transmitted in any form or by any means, electronic, mechanical, photocopying, recording or otherwise, without prior permission in writing from the publisher.

Printed and bound by
Antony Rowe Ltd
Bumper's Farm
Chippenham
Wiltshire SN14 6LH
United Kingdom

Important Note

If you believe you have a medical condition, the techniques outlined in this book should not be attempted without first consulting a doctor.

Some of the techniques in this book require a high level of fitness and suppleness and should not be attempted by anyone lacking such fitness.

Information given in this book is to the author's best knowledge and every effort has been made to ensure accuracy and safety but the author and publishers cannot accept any responsibility for any proceedings brought or instituted against any person or body as a result of the use or misuse of any techniques described in this book or any loss, injury or damage caused thereby.

Acknowledgements

Once again I am grateful for the support and editorial guidance of my friend and *sifu*, Alan Gibson.

Thanks also to Jamie Clubb for his helpful role as consultant to this second book in the series. I would also like to thank Dudley Walker for some excellent feedback on the performance of exercises, which has informed the second volume.

Special thanks to Peter Taylor-Medhurst and Continuo Creative, along with Ross Matthews for some fine photographic work.

A dozen copies of the first book went to my nearest and dearest. These people have variously picked me up, put me back together and set me straight when I've not been equal to the task myself. They remain the guides to the better parts of myself. Since that time I have been extremely fortunate to meet, work and play with so many fabulous people, I simply couldn't afford the print run to give you all a copy of the second volume. This is for you.

About Dr Matthew Mills

Matthew Mills obtained an Honours Degree in Physiology from the University of Leeds in 1989. He achieved his Masters Degree in Human and Applied Physiology from Kings College in 1990. Matthew was awarded his PhD from the Department of Medicine, University College London, in 1994. He went on to lecture in Sports Physiology and Health Promotion at the University of Birmingham, Department of Sport and Exercise.

In 1997 Matthew founded The Radical Health Strategy Group, drawing together diverse interests in workplace health promotion from the public and private sector. He led the group's contribution to the Government Green Paper, Our Healthier Nation in 1998. He remains active in the field, contributing to the Department for Work and Pensions and Health and Safety Executive Stress at Work initiative. Matthew is widely published on the subject of stress in the workplace and is regular conference speaker. Matthew consults for the leadership and cultural change consultants, Zoom and Capstone International Ltd, whose clients have included British American Racing (Formula One), Reuters, Johnson & Johnson, Prodrive (Rallying) and VISA. He has designed stress management and executive training packages for all of these clients.

Matthew has studied martial arts for nearly 20 years. He took up Karate at the age of 18, expanding his interest to study Eastern culture and Buddhism. Matthew took up Kung Fu during travels to Hong Kong and China, and has studied Wing Chun under the likes of Ip Chun, whose father taught Bruce Lee. He has developed executive training packages based on these studies, aimed at enhancing fitness, health and mental focus, delivered through Zoom (GB) Ltd.

Matthew is 40, father to one son – Ben – and lives in London.

Contents

Foreword by Alan Gibson	**10**
Foreword by Barry Holmes	**11**
1 Introduction	
Masters Mind and Body Metamorphosis	**13**
Mastery	
Developing your capacity to learn	**21**
2 Calm Focus	
Basic and advanced methods for creating the right frame of mind	**25**
3 Chi Kung Training	
Basic and advanced Chi Kung for stronger foundations	**55**
4 Stamina Training	
Basic and advanced Kung Fu exercises for endurance and weight control	**79**
5 Power Training	
Basic and advanced Wu Shu exercises for developing muscle strength	**105**
6 Special Situations	
Integration – personalising your program	**131**
Corporate Testimonials	**143**

Foreword by Alan Gibson

When Matthew asked me if I would write a foreword for his new book, I was pleased to accept; I consider it to be a significant addition to the world of health and exercise science. I applaud you on your choice and I am sure you will benefit from reading it more than just the once. Matthew has contributed to my own understanding of training and fitness, and I am happy to be able to add my little bit to his important work.

I first met Matthew when he came to me for advice on publishing his first book, Mind & Body Metamorphosis, we got on immediately and I am happy to say that we have become very good friends since this time. Matthew is not only highly qualified to talk about and advise on these matters but also trains using them himself. As a result, he expresses his ideas in a clear and well thought out manner, which in turn makes for easy reading and a clear understanding of the complex processes that underlie the ideas.

If you are fortunate enough to have Matthew's first volume already then there is no need for me to explain the effectiveness of this system. If not, you should perhaps consider obtaining it too, because although this book also serves as an introduction to the ideas and further explores more advanced training, the original is as good a foundation as you are likely to find anywhere.

Alan Gibson
Alan is the founder of The Wing Chun Federation www.wingchun.org.uk and the author of several books and DVDs about Ving Tsun.

Foreword by Barry Holmes

I had the privilege of writing a foreword for Matt's first book *Muscle Metamorphosis*, which I believed to be 'the' definitive guide for 'non-martial-artists' like myself to access some of the 'secrets' and benefits we see in those steely, hardened people who walk around with that air of confidence and calm like they know something you don't. (Not to mention the perfect abs!)

As much as I might fantasize, I am unlikely to move to Tibet to spend 10 years in a Buddhist monastery fasting, finding myself and maintaining a life of solitude and discipline. (A single day of fasting will send me screaming to the cupboard for a bag of nachos and big glass of white wine!)

What I don't want is to sacrifice my life to long, arduous, boring activities that are going to take a lifetime to perfect; what I want is results now, today, with minimum effort and maximum fun.

What I love about this book is how accessible Matt makes 'mystical profound truths', whether I am training to compete for my country (which I was last time I wrote my foreword) or just trying to stave off a beer gut and hypertension (which I am now!) The levels between white and black gave me a sense of progress whether I was just breathing better or holding my posture differently for 5 minutes. It's so good to write down in my diary what I HAVE done, rather than what I HAVEN'T!

Matt's approach has been to make things as succinct, simple and direct as possible without diluting the value. In fact you won't find any anecdotes, because the book is probably written in as few words as possible, which reminds me that I had better round off this intro.

Read, explore, test, play, enjoy – I did!

Barry Holmes
Director at Zoom

Chapter 1

Introduction

Masters Mind and Body Metamorphosis

"When you are master of your body, word and mind, you will rejoice in perfect serenity"

Shabkar

Introduction

I am a work in progress; rough around the edges, loose at the seams. Certainly I do not call myself Master too much at all. I was a chubby and insecure adolescent, desperately seeking something and not quite sure what it was. Adulthood found me equally rudderless, until the sky fell in to deposit a bout of suicidal depression and flirtation with alcoholism. Hardly the flashing white teeth and clear-eyed confidence of a self-help Guru. Nonetheless, perhaps the very raw material from which improvements grow?

The laboratory of the Kung Fu has been a great teacher to me. The stark test of fighting lays bare uncertainty and levels an unwavering finger at shortcomings in our perception of reality. The storehouse of philosophical wisdom underpinning Kung Fu illuminates a hypothesis to explain these flaws and provides a model through which they may be reconciled in the real World. Collected here, and in the first volume, are some of my hard-fought lessons.

I do not lay claim to any special knowledge or original insight. I'm not entirely sure what the ultimate goal of this research is meant to be. Every time I think I've got a firm conclusion, confounding new data appears. Perhaps this is 'The Way' martial artists keep banging on about – but I'm not certain. I do believe I have been improved by some very powerful techniques and, largely through those from whom I have learned, I am more than I was.

The empirical evidence does support the fact that these techniques work. They have stood the test of time, their value clearly reinforced by the obvious willingness to keep them alive. Direct experience demonstrates they have helped me, and countless others, prevail over testing times. However finished your personal project, and whatever your goals, I am confident applying the information contained here will help you find your answers.

The roots of Mind and Body Metamorphosis
Opinions vary on the origins of Chinese boxing, or Kung Fu. Systematic methods for training unarmed combat were probably first developed for soldiers by the military.

Training included not only fighting techniques, but also physical and mental conditioning to endure in battle. Many fighting systems would have been developed among rival armies. Tested against each other in combat, only the most effective systems would produce survivors to pass them on. Over the centuries the best techniques for training and fighting evolved into a highly efficient, scientific training system, putting mind and body in a state of readiness for confrontation.

On leaving the military, Kung Fu exponents taught their skills to family members. Handed down from generation to generation, fighting ability could be decisive in resolving disputes and reinforcing a particular clan's position in the social order. As a result, Kung Fu training techniques and skills became jealously guarded family secrets. Shrouded in social tradition and secrecy, speculation around the abilities of Kung Fu practitioners often transformed them and their deeds into legend. It was often in a clan's interest to perpetuate these myths, a phenomenon which continues to this day, to create awe and wonder in the mind of a potential opponent. Beneath these distortions, the effectiveness of this training system is evidenced by the fact it continues to thrive today.

An objective examination of Kung Fu training reveals a progressive and powerful conditioning system, grounded in solid scientific principles. *Master's Mind and Body* presents Kung Fu training, and its benefits, from this pragmatic perspective.

Eastern wisdom for the western world
Consistent with this idea, Kung Fu does not in fact mean martial art, boxing or even fighting. The term Kung Fu, which does not have a simple translation into English, really means attainment. Developing fighting ability, or martial Kung, is only one element of Kung Fu. Attainment can also be expressed through learning the ability to remain calm under trying circumstances, to maintain physical constitution

against the effects of age or inactivity, or simply improving ourselves through better knowledge of our own abilities. While life and death fights are fortunately rare these days, the latter forms of attainment make Kung Fu as relevant today as ever – maybe more so.

Eastern strategies for fitness

The last decade or so has seen an explosion of fitness training as a means to better physical condition and health. It is a fair question, therefore, to ask whether Mind and Body Metamorphosis will help you become fit. An even more important question is just what we mean by 'fitness'.

Fitness is a fairly vague term, usually taken to mean something about being lean, muscular and able to run a mile or two without too much trouble. Fitness for one person however, may mean little to someone else. A runner is fit if they can endure for miles at a time, but would probably not be fit to enter a weightlifting competition, as their training is not geared to the demands of lifting heavy weights. Fitness is more properly defined by the demands of what we are doing and our readiness to meet them.

Readiness for the everyday

Whether you are a specialist in a particular sport or not, we all share the demands of daily life. The last hundred years in particular has seen an unprecedented transition in the way we live. We have moved from a rural economy, in which most of us performed manual work, toward largely sedentary occupations in which the principal burden is the accelerating pace of technological change. Every indication suggests as a direct result we are becoming increasingly anxious and depressed, overweight and under-muscled, prematurely aged and vulnerable to disease.

Introduction

Mind and Body Metamorphosis for everyday readiness

Everyday readiness, and the training to attain it, are defined by the demands of our lives. The following list could doubtless be expanded – evidence suggests our readiness attainment strategy should target:

Self-confidence	maintaining a positive view of ourselves
Weight control	maintaining body fat at reasonable levels
Age prevention	maintaining the strength of muscle and bone
Disease prevention	maintaining the health of internal organs such as the heart

Mind and Body Metamorphosis delivers these objectives with a training syllabus systematically directed towards:

Mental relaxation	the ability to enjoy life and see things calmly
Breathing & mobility	the ability to move joints freely and breath fully
Stamina	the ability to keep going with energy to spare
Strength	the ability to carry and lift with ease

The logic of such a syllabus or routine is almost self-evident, and there are various exercise systems based on it. A typical exercise program will however, usually fail to deliver on its promise! This is not necessarily the fault of the strategy itself, but rather its inability to keep the participant interested and involved. The effects of exercise are short-lived, lasting hours or days, and only continued participation will deliver lasting results. Most fitness and health promotion programs retain only 5-10% of entrants, so few enjoy much benefit. In addition to the basic elements of a readiness attainment, the strategy must itself deliver the key elements which evidence suggests will keep us interested. In addition to its basic objectives, the advantages of Mind and Body Metamorphosis are:

Inclusive	anyone can join in
Confidence	systematically developing a positive attitude
Challenge	enough difficulty to grow, but not put us off
Progression	seeing and enjoying improvements
Variety	enough scope to change the strategy
Enjoyment	scope to imagine, play and have fun
Convenience	no special equipment or clothing required
Portability	perform anywhere
Flexibility	adaptable to time and personal constraints
Adaptability	applicable to our own objectives
Range	good for groups or those who would exercise alone

Mind and Body Metamorphosis and lifelong readiness

The exercises are arranged in a rough order of difficulty in a sequence designed to develop a relaxed mind, positive focus, enhanced stamina and enhanced muscular power. This is not dissimilar to the natural evolution of Kung Fu itself. So, in many cases each series of exercises forms the foundation for easy progression to the next. While they appear novel at first, each exercise is thoroughly illustrated with easy-to-follow steps.

The Kung Fu system implicitly includes elements to help us remain encouraged and keep practising over the long term. I have included interesting variations for many exercises, along with advanced alternatives and routines for specific objectives. These are all graded by colour (like the belt systems in Judo and Karate) so as you can choose exercises appropriate for your own ability or level of comfort. Almost anyone can therefore engage in these exercises at some level and observe progression.

I have included elements explicitly aimed at breaking down barriers to practice. The system of exercises is sufficiently flexible to adapt to almost any need, location or time constraint, and I have provided guidelines on how to do so. Further, realising the minds' direction is essential to success, there are specific guidelines on how to preserve your enthusiasm and prevent the urge to give up. The resulting system is direct, complete and effective.

Advanced Mind and Body Metamorphosis

This book builds on the ideas presented in the original volume. The Advanced Program is delivered over a 12 week period, progressing through increasingly demanding stages from White to Black. As we master one series of skills, another is added at the most basic level. Each lesson is designed to help you understand your objective, provide the best techniques to reach it, and develop the foundation for further growth. Each chapter revisits basic training principles before presenting advanced conditioning concepts. The Advanced Program syllabus uses new skills that greatly enhance those you have already acquired.

Each part of the syllabus develops key skills to get the most out of the following stages. This itinerary assumes you have attained basic conditioning putting into practice the ideas in the original volume. For those who are new to the Mind and Body Metamorphosis approach (even if you are well conditioned), I'd suggest a break-in period following the six-week, White level, Entry Program. This will provide an invaluable grounding of basic techniques on which to build when you move on.

Entry Program

Week	Calm Focus	Chi Kung Training	Stamina Training	Power Training
1	White			
2	White	White		
3	White	White	White	
4	White	White	White	
5	White	White	White	White
6	White	White	White	White

Mental focus and a positive attitude are critical to success, and the syllabus begins with exercises to put us in the right frame of mind to get the most out of training. The Advanced Program builds these positive thinking skills into an upbeat world view using philosophical concepts from Buddhism. Advanced Chi Kung develops basic breathing techniques into a sophisticated set of exercises, called The Eight Pieces of Brocade, designed to systematically enhance coordination between mind and body. This establishes the essential foundation for advanced stamina training, combining traditional Form and Mind Boxing with the most up-to-date techniques. Developing muscular power begins halfway through the course, having acclimatized ourselves to a markedly increased exercise intensity. The Advanced program takes another quantum leap in exercise intensity and expression of muscular power through Hard Kung training.

Advanced Program

Week	Calm Focus	Chi Kung Training	Stamina Training	Power Training
1	Yellow	Yellow	White	White
2	Red	Red	White	White
3	Blue	Red	Yellow	White
4	Black	Blue	Red	White
5	-	Blue	Red	White
6	-	Black	Blue	White
7	-	-	Blue	Yellow
8	-	-	Blue	Red
9	-	-	Black	Red
10	-	-	-	Blue
11	-	-	-	Blue
12	Black	Black	Black	Black

The Master's Mind and Body program is inescapably more demanding and sophisticated than its predecessor. Your commitment will manifest in significantly higher conditioning and deeper insight into your training, translating to greater leverage in reaching your goals. The laurel of mastery is not without cost and, as in most areas of life, our achievements are earned by the effort and sacrifice we are willing to make. But then, as so often proves the case, something simply given has no value.

Mastery:
developing your capacity to learn

Explanation

A book cannot possibly replace tuition from a qualified instructor. The subtle nuances of form and function inherent to Kung Fu can only be appreciated under the watchful gaze of the Master. Most of us would accept this as an axiom. This begs the question, who does the Master learn from?

The Master has learned to teach themselves. Examining a new martial arts book for instance, the Master will not simply go through the motions and try to mimic the movements. Rather, they will question the purpose of each movement, its function and how it can evolve. When attempting to perform the movement, the Master pays attention to how it feels. Focusing on the sensations in their muscle and joints, they evaluate each subsequent attempt against the form and function they are trying to achieve. Through trial, error and sensitivity to the feedback from their own body, the Master eventually hones the technique.

Coaching of some kind is essential of any form of self-improvement. Without objective feedback you have no yardstick for improvement and your progress will always be limited. This is what the Masters provide when you train with them. The ability to independently question, critically evaluate and adapt – to coach and learn for ourselves – is a central aim of Kung Fu. This is the key skill the Master encourages in their student, and represents the point when we can achieve Mastery for ourselves. Not only are these skills simple and easy to learn, you don't have to follow a Master for 20 years before they are revealed to you.

Practice

1. Attitude is everything. Approach learning any new skill with a positive, confident frame of mind. None of the skills in this volume are beyond you, if you put in the work. So, believe you can do it.

2. It's easier to learn a new movement when you understand its function. You have already taught yourself a vast repertoire of movement skills, from learning to crawl to standing up and walking. These skills are based on a limited range of basic movements from which you can borrow when learning a new skill. Examine the new skill and consider its function. Does it share similarities with something else you already know how to do? This will help you place each movement in context and draw from your existing repertoire.

3. If you can imagine how to perform a movement, it becomes easier to do it. Visualise performing the movement you are trying to learn. Borrow from something similar you already know how to do. This can be the full movement or just a component. Imagine how a successful movement will feel.

4. You can learn several simple movements faster than one complicated one. Break a new skill down into smaller components that you can practise in isolation. If you're learning a complicated arm movement for example, you can probably break it down into a series of simpler components, which you can then practise separately. Practise each movement in order – with a small break in between. Gradually reduce the gap between each component and build up to the full movement.

5. Be sensitive to feedback. As you perform your new skill, pay attention to feedback from your body. Focus on how the movement feels; how your joints move and muscle tension changes. Try small adjustments during subsequent attempts and note if this improves or detracts from the feeling of the movement. If a particular sensation, such as tension in a particular muscle, grabs your attention, stay focused on it until you notice something more interesting.

6 Start slowly. It's easier to pay attention to feedback when your movements are slow and relaxed. Gradually build up speed and power as you acquire competence with each movement.

7 Inform the learning process. Your experience practising a new skill can be used to improve the quality and speed of learning. Paying attention to feedback from your muscles and joints can be used to make your visualisation more accurate and effective. More accurate visualisation will help you better understand the component movements and the function of a new skill. In turn, this experience will reinforce your progress and confidence.

Variations

Another useful yardstick for learning is performance. If you are becoming more effective, it stands to reason your learning has been successful. This does not mean to say you are performing a skill in exactly the same way as someone else. In the final analysis, however, effective expression of our skills is the ultimate objective, not the superficial reproduction of pictures on a page.

Benefits

The learning process described here systematically illustrates the natural abilities you have at your disposal. Once you have acquainted yourself with this process, mastery of any new skill will become a matter of course.

Chapter 2

Calm Focus

Basic and advanced methods for creating the right frame of mind

"You can't stop the waves,
but you can learn to surf"
Joseph Goldstein

Calm Focus 2.0
Calm Focus – Basic and advanced methods for creating the right frame of mind

What is focus?

Some people always get what they want, while others constantly seem to miss the mark. The difference between them is often the ability of successful people to focus the power of their mind on achieving their goals. We can define focus as attention on a specific goal. The idea also has deeper connotations of directing our thoughts, will and actions – the power of the mind – to reaching that goal. The study of the mind pre-dates written history, from the first time one human being wondered why another was acting this way or that way. Perhaps later this prompted the questioner to ask the same questions of themselves – why am I doing this and how do I feel about it? The scientific discipline of psychology was born of these questions and is a relative newcomer on the scene, having only been around a hundred years or so. As such, it is a little short on definitive answers about why we think, act and feel the way we do. There are however, some common patterns in human behaviour that give us clues as to why some people can successfully reach their goals, and others can't.

Feel, think and act positively

When you find yourself in the company of focused people it becomes very clear that they know what they want. Whether it's losing weight, succeeding in business or making a relationship work, they can see how to get there and feel confident they can do it. When you talk with them, focused people tend to be positive and upbeat. Their enthusiasm is often infectious; it carries them, and those around them, over and around seemingly insurmountable problems to great achievements. Focused people seem to get lucky, but on closer inspection it becomes clear they make their luck with careful and systematic planning of how they will reach their goals. The benchmarks and milestones of success are clearly laid out, with specific actions and skills practised at each stage to ensure the final outcome. When things go wrong – as they surely will – focused people don't turn the situation into a drama. They view events in a calm, realistic way and positively try to turn things around. Even when they go off the rails and lose focus – and who hasn't? – this is not a reason to quit. The lessons are learned from failure and focus returns even stronger! In short, focused people have learned a valuable lesson – how you think affects how you feel, affects how you act, effects what you get. Psychology has been successful in giving us a way to systematically improve all of these elements of focus.

Advanced focus principles

Focused people have built up an arsenal of positive-thinking skills. These equip them with powerful tools to ward off daily distractions and upsets, and stay on track to reach their objectives.

A potential limitation of positive-thinking skills is that they are situational and reactive. They help us deal with events, moment by moment, as they arise. The most successful and focused people have also learned to place positive-thinking skills in the context of a optimistic world view. This provides a framework for seeing life that helps them to stay happy and maintain an upbeat attitude, no matter what its trials and tribulations.

There have been many attempts, philosophical and theological, to develop a coherent strategy for global harmony. Several of these have become associated with the martial arts. This may have come about through fighters manufacturing an acceptable link to sell their skills to the public, or to provide a palliative against the inevitable, emotional pressure of daily combat. Tested under such circumstances, any successful philosophical approach must have relevance to our stressful, modern lives.

The philosophy most commonly associated with the Chinese Kung Fu is Buddhism. Without excluding any existing beliefs you may hold, the underlying teachings point to a happier and calmer perspective on life by systematically learning to see the world – and act within it – in a positive, realistic way. This is an ideal framework within which to hang and enhance your positive-thinking skills.

Benefits of learning to focus

Focus exercises can, and should, be performed as often as possible. Developing the habit of positive focus will deliver:

Less stress, consistently better mood and health.

More energy, enthusiasm and effort toward your goals.

Better relations with those around you, which may also help you reach your goals.

Guidelines for developing focus

- Practise as often as you can to make positive focus as habit.
- Practise with an open mind.
- Take the time to master each exercise. There is no rush.
- Begin your practice in a quiet, peaceful place.
- Once you have mastered the techniques, the best time to practise is whenever you can.
- Try and apply your practice to everyday situations and constantly improving yourself.

Using these exercises

Learning to create focus and motivation focus is a complex skill based on a series of relatively simple building blocks. The following pages lead you through the steps to developing a positive outlook on your goals and how to reach them. Work through each step, being sure to understand it before proceeding to the next. Leaving any step out weakens the overall effect. Like learning to walk, reshaping patterns of thinking ingrained over a lifetime takes time and you can expect to fall over a few times. These are amongst the most difficult skills in this volume, but once mastered you will take one of the greatest steps toward realising your goals.

Calm Focus 2.1
Calm Focus basics

Explanation

We've all had the experience of life getting on top of us. Too much to do and not enough time. It is very difficult to focus under these conditions and all too easy to lose track of where we are and what we're doing. When it all gets a bit much you just have to close your eyes, take a deep breath and smile. A deep breath activates a series of reflexes slowing breathing, our heart rate and helps us calm down. Feedback from our facial muscles, making us look happy, actually makes us feel happier. Overall this puts us in the right frame of mind to address the problem.

In developing calm focus it's important to recognise that the way we feel has a profound influence on how we think and act. For example, if you've had a bad day, you may well end up feeling low; you begin thinking the World is against you and collapse on the couch for a fairly unproductive night of TV. So, when we feel down we tend to think in an unrealistically negative way and our behaviour may follow the same pattern.

Fortunately, this process can be put into reverse. If we can think positively, we will feel better and be more likely to act positively. This will help us stay focused on our goals and less likely to get sidetracked by problems. The skill of positive thinking – keeping it real – is a powerful tool that can be picked up quickly and once learned soon becomes a habit.

Performance

1 Find somewhere quiet where you won't be disturbed. Then sit or lay down in a relaxed posture. Close your eyes and take a long, deep breath. Repeat a few times until you start to relax.

2 Focus your attention on your legs and feel them relax. If it helps you to say or think the word 'relax' – or some other word that works for you – do so.

3 Keeping your eyes closed, slowly shift focus up your body, feeling all your muscles relax. Take a few more long, slow, deep breaths.

4 Keeping your eyes closed, and continuing to breathe slowly, try to create an image in your mind of somewhere you find pleasant and relaxing. This could be a beach, a wood, a garden – whatever works for you. Try and add some colour to the scene, feeling warm sunshine on your face, smelling flowers – once again, whatever helps you.

5 When you're ready, open your eyes, have a bit of a stretch and smile.

6 Now, grab a piece of paper and a pen. Write down what happened that made you feel low.

7 Write down some words to describe how you felt, eg, upset, down, frustrated, angry…

8 Write down what you thought when you felt this way, eg, 'I've failed', 'I should be able to do this', 'how dare they do this to me!'…

9 Now have a good look at what you were thinking. Often, our thinking becomes unrealistically negative when we're down or upset.

10 Write down what you ended up doing when you thought this way eg, 'couldn't be bothered', 'had an argument about it'… When we feel negative, our actions often follow and are often unproductive.

11 Now write down what a good friend (someone who knows you, likes you and is sympathetic to you) would say to you to help you feel better if the same thing happened again.

12 The statement from a friend is likely to be more realistic, positive and sympathetic to us. Hearing this statement makes us feel better. So, every time a situation emerges which makes you feel down, go through this process. Be sure to write things down at first, as this helps ingrain the skill. After a few weeks of practice, it will come naturally.

> **Example:**
> **What happened:** I put on a few pounds.
> **How did I feel:** Guilty, frustrated, irritated.
> **What did I think:** What a failure – I'm turning into a fat blob!
> **What did I do:** Forgot exercise today. Watched TV instead.
> **What would a friend say:** OK, so you put on a few pounds. That doesn't make you a failure, it happens. Work out and watch your diet for a while and you'll lose it. I know you can do it.
> The second statement is both more positive AND realistic – keeps it real.
> The second statement makes me feel better and more likely to take productive action.

Variations

You can practise this sequence almost anywhere. You can be sitting at your desk at work, on the train or any time at home. If you have a friend who will work through some examples with you that really helps, as you'll be getting actual feedback from them.

Benefits

The ability to relax is an amazingly useful and beneficial skill. As we'll see later, a calm mind helps us think more clearly, making us more focused on our goals and effective in reaching them. If you can stay positive and keep it real, you take a giant leap towards reaching whatever goal you set your mind to. Equally, most of us would rather feel positive and happy than down and negative. Therefore, changing the way you think can radically improve the quality of your life. Investing a few moments in using these skills clearly provides massive benefits for many areas of our lives.

Level White

Calm Focus 2.2
Success-building basics

Explanation

Many goals in life can at first seem insurmountable. Almost no obstacle will stop someone who believes 'I can!' The trick to developing this attitude is to create a self-image that is not only positive, but also invulnerable to the winds of change or fickle opinions of others. While the world around us may never be certain, our self-belief can become an unshakeable positive force. Focused people have also learned that the key to staying positive and interested in their goals is to break them down into smaller, achievable steps. Each step builds the feeling 'I can do it', increasing commitment to the next.

The process relies on being realistic about what you want, what you have to do to achieve it and how long it is likely to take. Another important element of self-belief is being able to see ourselves able to accomplish our goals. When we can conceive ourselves as successful we increase our chances of fulfilling that vision. Visualisation serves as a kind of rehearsal for the real thing. When it comes to the real thing, our performance will be better.

Performance

1 Think how a good friend would describe you and write this down in a few sentences. Then break down the statement into the separate items that make you feel good about yourself. Eg, 'I feel good about me because… I'm a nice guy… and I always try my best.'

2 Split the items up into two groups on the basis of those things you have to achieve something to justify and those you'd have regardless of the outcome. For example, you have to do something to justify 'I am successful at work'. You 'try your best' regardless.

3 Now write out a sentence about yourself as if a good friend were describing you based only on the items you satisfy regardless of what you do. For example, if you feel good about yourself because you try your best, you'll be positive despite the outcome of your effort. This statement gives you an unconditional, positive statement about yourself that you can believe in and feel good about no matter what happens. Write it down. No one's opinion can change this, and the only measure you have to live up to is your own.

4 Having built a robust attitude, think about the goal you want to achieve and write it down – this makes it concrete and real. You'll be amazed how simply writing your goal down makes a difference. Think about what progress you could realistically make over the course of a month, then write down weekly benchmarks toward this goal. Write down what you'd have to do on a week-by-week, and daily, basis to hit your benchmark.

5 Use your benchmarks to show gaps in your knowledge. If you're not sure exactly how to achieve them, find out more about what you're doing. You can also use this system to show you how to recover if you go off the rails. If you lapse from your daily or weekly plan, you will know how far behind your benchmarks you can expect to be. You'll be able to take a realistic view of whether you can catch up or if you have to adjust your benchmarks. Stick to your daily plan and review progress against your benchmarks every week. If progress is not as expected, the fact that you've been systematic means you can easily feed that experience into next week's plan and improve your results.

6 Find somewhere quiet where you won't be disturbed. Close your eyes and take a few deep breaths and relax. Now focus your mind on your goal, whatever that may be. Try to imagine yourself when you have reached it. Create an image of where you will be, what it will look like and how you will feel. Add as much colour as possible by imagining who will be there, what will they say to you, what other benchmarks of success you will see, feel, smell and touch.

7 Now focus on an important skill you require to reach your goal. This may be a form of exercise, a work task or other activity. In your mind, run through performing that task perfectly. Imagine what a perfect outcome looks and feels like. Think through the task again in slow motion. Try to feel every movement or gesture as if it were actually happening.

Variations

You can take the step-by-step success process to almost any level you want. You can plan down to the last detail, or, so long as you stick to the broad principles, you don't have to be obsessive to get what you want. To begin with, you may find visualisation easier if you imagine watching yourself perform a skill or activity. Just like watching TV, most of us are used to watching others in this way.

Benefits

Thinking of ourselves in a positive way is one of the most powerful means to feel consistently upbeat. Previously negative situations will have less impact on us, while enhanced self-belief readily translates from improved motivation into higher achievements. Taking a systematic approach to your goals immensely improves your chances of reaching them. Being rewarded by success on a regular basis is a great way to keep you focused on your goals. Visualisation is also a very powerful tool. If you can seriously imagine yourself succeeding, you will.

Calm Focus 2.3
The universe is not out to get you

Explanation

Sometimes nothing seems to work out right. Despite your very best efforts, what can go wrong does go wrong. It's almost as if there is a grand design to trip you up at every turn. Naturally enough, you eventually throw your hands up in despair and ask 'why me?!'

This very question implies a belief we are somehow special, and we should expect preferential treatment from life. Clearly, this is a rather unrealistic and distorted view of the world. From this rather egocentric perspective, it's very difficult to explain why things have gone wrong. In fact, if you really are the centre of the Universe, it follows that when things go wrong for you, events must have conspired to deliberately set you up for a fall – The Universe must be out to get you!

Clinging to the delusion we are special puts us up against influences utterly beyond our control. It can be difficult enough getting a handle on things close to home, let alone how distant events will affect us. The more you try to control them, the more frustrated you'll become. Put frankly, going toe-to-toe with The Universe, you just don't have a chance!

The plain truth is that the Universe ebbs and flows with absolutely no regard for our daily trivia. We are all part of the Grand order; a unique part it must be granted, but not its focus. When you accept the more realistic view of being part of something bigger than yourself and going with the flow, this puts the Universe on your side – now you're on the winning team.

Performance

1 Grab a pen and some paper, or use the Notes section at the back of this volume.

2 Think back to a day when everything seemed to go wrong.

3 At the top of the page write a few words to explain what happened, such as 'It was raining and I couldn't find my umbrella, I missed the bus and got soaked, then I couldn't meet my deadline at the office'.

4 Write some single words to express how this made you feel, like 'Upset, frustrated, angry…' and so on.

5 Now write down some of the things you were thinking when this happened, such as 'This is really unfair, why does this keep happening to me?!'

6 Take a long look at your statements. Ask yourself, are they a truly accurate reflection of what REALLY happened?

7 Try to pick out the bits of your statement that aren't an absolutely accurate description of what happened. For example, if you wrote 'this keeps happening', is it true that this happens every single time?

8 Now try rewriting these statements in a more realistic and accurate way. For instance 'Fair has nothing to do with it. It's just one of those things, just this time. Actually, when I look at this calmly, things usually work out OK'.

9 Finally, compare both statements and ask yourself which one makes you feel better?

Variations

You've heard of the butterfly effect? A butterfly flaps its wings in South America, setting in motion a chain of events that lead to a hurricane in the Caribbean. This is a metaphor used to illustrate an effect called chaos, which basically explains how small actions now can ramify to much bigger effects downstream. It's also another useful way to think about events and how they affect you. There are literally billions of butterflies flapping away and affecting the course of your day. They don't mean you any harm, and you couldn't stop them if you wanted to, so why fight it?

Benefits

Learning to go with the flow not only takes much of the struggle out of life, but also begins the journey toward a more realistic and overwhelmingly positive world view.

Calm Focus 2.4
The truth of the matter

Explanation

Bodhidharma was an Indian Prince who lived in the lap of luxury, sheltered form the outside World. When he finally ventured out from the gilded confines of his palace, he was horrified to see suffering in all its forms. He was so disturbed by all this that he is supposed to have left his wife and children to sit in contemplation under a Bodhi tree for seven years. In one of those 'Ah-ha!' moments, he reached upon enlightenment, understood the problem and developed a solution: The Noble Truths.

Bodhidharma reasoned something like this: In life, there is also suffering, such as personal loss, ageing, illness or death. This is the deal, and part of the natural order. These become sources of unhappiness when we won't go with the flow and accept them for what they are. There is a solution and an end to unhappiness. This comes when we accept things for what they are and stop grasping after what we'd like them to be. Q.E.D.

Performance

1 All of us, at some time, have experienced a loss of some kind. This could be anything from a relationship to a job, from our looks to a favourite mug that broke. Write down what it was for you.

2 Write a few words to express how you felt, such as 'upset, frustrated, angry', or any combination that best describes how you felt.

3 Then, write a few words to describe any thoughts that you had at the same time. Such as 'What a disaster, how could this happen to me?!', or 'This is the absolute end, I'll never get over this!' Whatever it was, write what best describes how you were thinking.

4 Now write a few words about what it was you actually lost, be it companionship, security, pride or just a mug that reminded you of a blinding day out you had once.

5 Take a moment to think back to the event. What did your best friend say to you to try and cheer you up? Write it down and consider how it made you feel better?

6 A friend tends to say things in a much more supportive and positive way. 'It's not the end of the World' deftly points out that matters usually haven't deteriorated too badly. Many of us gauge our thoughts and opinions on those of others, particularly our close friends. This helps us adjust our own feelings toward something more realistic.

7 Importantly, our friends will often point out that we are not the only ones who have suffered a rainy day. For instance, break-ups are often accompanied by old warhorses like 'There's plenty more fish in the sea' and 'you've still got me!' This reminds us that these events happen to many other people, all the time. Things never seem quite so bleak when you realise we are all in the same boat together.

Variations

When things don't go the way you'd planned, it's easy to indulge in a bit of self-pity. This is rarely productive and almost never helps you get over it, and move on. Another way to shift our perspective on events is to try and look at them in context. Try listing out all the people you know well. Tick off any who you know for certain haven't had a similar hard time or personal crisis. First off, you'll doubtless find you're in good company. Second, you'll probably identify someone who's been there before and can help you out.

Benefits

For all the fabulous bits, life also comes with some inevitable downside. It can be very easy to believe our own experience is unique; a misconception that just seems to make things worse. The reality is that we are ALL in the same boat. It might be sinking, but we'll be going down together!

Calm Focus 2.5
The tighter you grip

Explanation

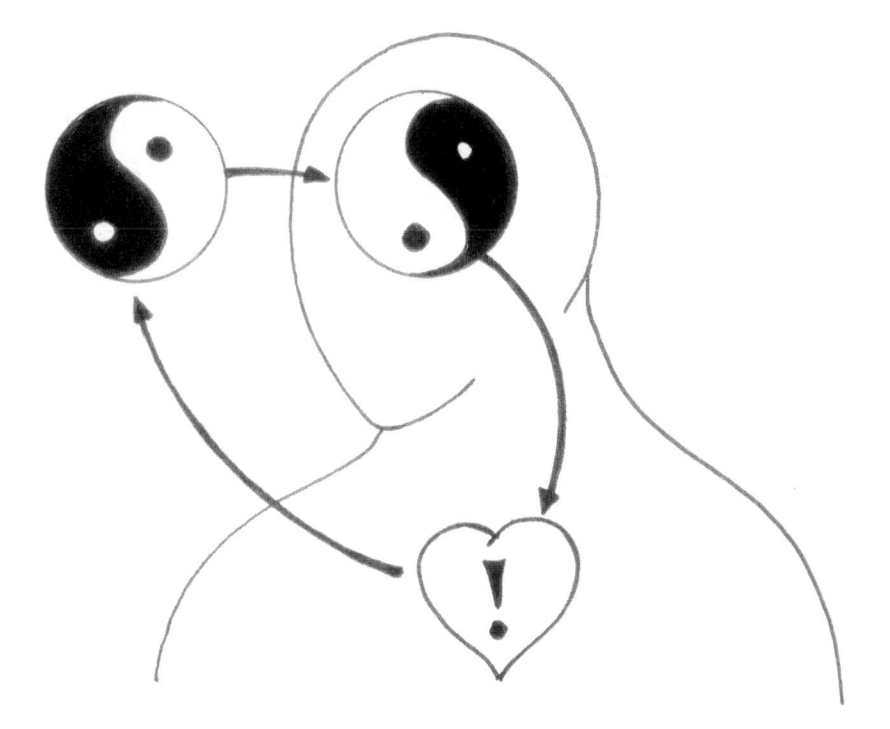

Everything changes. You, your relationships, everything you do and everything you own is in a constant state of flux. None of us is exempt. Sitting under his Bodhi tree, watching the passing seasons, Bodhidharma also noticed that change was part of the grand order. Ruminating on the nature of impermanence, Bodhidharma figured it was clearly an important factor explaining suffering. It is our own impermanence that eventually leads us to grow old, become ill and one day pass off this mortal coil – in short, to suffer. Change is only half the story, however, and the mysterious equations of happiness must also factor in our reaction to it. Typically, this is deny it is happening altogether. We often see things that make us happy, whether they are relationships, activities or possessions, as if they will always be there and always be the same. When we are faced with change, such as during a break-up, job loss, or as we age, there may be a widening gap between the things that once made us happy and our current circumstances. Rather than accept the reality of change, we'll often hang on to the illusion of what once made us happy. Bodhidharma described this as 'Grasping'. The tighter we grasp at something, the more frustrated we become – the more we suffer – as it continues to change.

Performance

1 Go back to the previous exercises. Re-read the examples and your own responses again.

2 Focus on the positive and realistic statement a friend may give you when you are down.

3 Think back to a time when this has happened to you. Often we will argue with someone trying to make us feel better. These are called Automatic Negative Thoughts. From a Buddhist perspective, you could think of them coming from our attempt to grasp after something that used to make us happy, but has now changed.

4 In the example below, Automatic Negative Thoughts have been included. Try and think of a time you may have thought like this and how it made you feel.

5 When you practise trying to be positive, realistic and focused doubts will crop up. Usually they will follow an attempt to think in a more positive way. Automatic Negative Thoughts often manifest themselves as fear and anxiety: eg, 'I can be successful, and move on from this – yes, but what if I fail?'

6 The best way to deal with these fears and doubts is to accept them for what they are. This takes away their power and leaves us able to feel positive.

7 Simply add a statement accepting fears and doubts and they'll soon disappear. eg,. 'I can be successful and move on from this – yes, but what if I fail?' and so, 'I am bothered by the idea of failing, and scared about what change will mean, but everybody is and I'm no different. I will try my best regardless'.

Example

What happened: A job ended in redundancy.

How did I feel: Angry, anxious, upset, scared.

What did I think: What a disaster, I'll never get another job now!

What did I do: Get drunk with mates.

What would a friend say: Sorry mate. I feel terrible for you. But listen, don't go blaming yourself. There are loads of reasons a job gets wound up. It just didn't work out this time. You're hard working and reliable, so you'll get snapped up by another company in no time.

Doubt: Yes, but, I can't believe this has happened. It was a great job. What did I do wrong?!

Accept it: I'm scared of being out of work – everyone is! The universe doesn't revolve around me, and the job market changes. I can get another good job if I try.

Accepting the doubt not only renders it ineffective, it actually makes keeping it real more powerful.

Variations

This process is much easier with a friend to kick ideas around. Whatever change you may be facing, it's easier with someone else. Friends are not only supportive, but often offer a fresh perspective. They may just have some ideas on how to adapt to change that you haven't thought of.

Benefits

Change affects all of us. This is not to say its consequences are always negative or that sometimes you shouldn't fight for what makes you happy. Grasping relentlessly after something that is changing beyond our control simply sets us up to suffer. Being realistic and accepting change makes the outcome, whatever it is, easier to live with.

Variations

Practise opening and closing the stances 10 times or more in succession. Practise holding the stance for a minute or more, keeping your legs tensed and breathing steadily as you do. Practise launching a series of punches at different heights. Try cycling the hands in the reverse direction. The rear hand comes forward, under the lead arm as you pull it back.

Benefits

Few exercises target the upper body for stamina training and even fewer will tax them like chain punching. Equally, you'll quickly find practising this stance toning up your thighs and backside.

Calm Focus

Level Red

Calm Focus 2.6
Waking up

Explanation

How many times have you found yourself daydreaming about the past, only to be rudely awakened by something suddenly happening around you? At one time or another we all find ourselves lamenting something we've said or done – or something we didn't. Conversely, how many times have you been completely excited about a future event, only to be totally let down when it actually arrives? Either way, we've all been affected now by something that's long since gone or hasn't even happened.

Bodhidarma likened this kind of thinking to a delusion, because it's essentially all going on in our head. Whether we're grasping after what once made us happy, or we believe might in the future, it happens nowhere but our own mind. We're essentially making the choice to suffer here and now, through the way we think about the world. Changing how we think, therefore, can also change how we feel here and now.

Bodhidharma suggested this was one of the keys to being happy more of the time. Basically, stop letting your mind wander off, grasping after the past or into the future. Practice focusing on reality as it is, rather than how we might like to be, here and now. He dubbed this process awakening.

Performance

1 Think back to an event that left you feeling bothered or upset. Write down what it was and how long ago it happened.

2 Write a few words about how it made you feel and the kind of thoughts that come to mind.

3 Divide the rest of the page into two columns.

4 Head one column 'When I think about this'. Then write down how it affects you here and now when you think about what happened. Consider how it affects your mood, thoughts and way you behave. For instance 'When I think about this… My mood sinks, I become grumpy and tend to snap at people and upset them as well'. Try and think of as many ways of how you're affected as possible. Add up how many points you made.

5 Head the next column 'If I didn't think about this'. Write down all the benefits to your mood, thoughts and actions. For instance 'If I didn't think about this… I'd be happier more of the time, I wouldn't snap at people, we'd all get on better'. Once again, think of as many ramifications as possible and add up all the points you make.

6 Now compare the points you made under each column. Is it more or less valuable to you, right here and now, thinking about something that upset you in the past? Be sure and write your answer down.

7 Then look at how long ago this event happened. How long has it affected you? Is it more or less valuable to you, right here and now, to continue letting this event affect you. Once again, write your answer down.

Variations

This value exercise works just as well with an expectation that has not been met at some point. It's also very useful to work through this exercise with a friend who can give you feedback on your answers.

Benefits

We've all got baggage. You can't simply dump it, but you can choose how you carry it. Grasping is pretty much like dragging around a suitcase full of bricks – you're going to suffer. When you wake up you suddenly realise you've had a 24-hour porter all along and life can be a whole lot easier.

Calm Focus 2.7
Moving standing still

Explanation

For most of us it is second nature to worry about something we wished we'd done, or should do. Our minds can become so full of anxieties it not only becomes very easy to miss all the good things going on in the present, but also impossible to see a light at the end of the tunnel. Moments of calm focus tend to sneak up on us, with few of us able to plan them effectively, to the extent that they are always a surprise. Waking up requires practice.

Calm, focused awareness is developed through the practice of meditation. This means nothing more than focusing intently on something. In a Buddhist context it is a method to learn being totally aware of the here and now. Our aim is to develop a tranquil state of mind, focusing our awareness on reality as it is, rather than grasping after things the way we'd like them to be.

There are a variety of different methods to practise meditation. Most of us are familiar with the idea of seated meditation, just like Boddhidharma practised under his Bodhi tree. Here you might focus your mind on the present by counting your breaths. Every time you find yourself grasping at some thought from the past or into the future, you re-focus your mind and start counting all over. Breath counting is only one form of practice, and you could legitimately use anything that helps focus your attention. Painting, reading, gardening, walking, and the practice of Kung Fu itself are equally as useful.

Performance

1 Find somewhere you can sit comfortably without being interrupted. Close your eyes and take a couple of deep breaths. Try to relax and clear you mind of any worries.

2 Focus your mind on your breathing. Follow your breath as it comes in through your nose, and down into your chest. Feel your chest and tummy move in and out as your breath.

3 Now start counting your breaths. Start at one and work up. Every time another thought comes to mind, acknowledge it, let it go and then return to counting from one again. Don't become discouraged if you often find yourself distracted. Calm focus takes a long time to develop and for many it takes years just to get past counting to two or three! Also, the object is not to reach counting to ten without distraction. Counting is just a method to practise, not an end in itself.

4 When you've got the hang of it, try using abdominal breathing as described in the next chapter. This type of breathing will help you relax further and deepen your focus.

5 You don't have to sit in meditation. If you feel more comfortable standing – or if that's when you've got the opportunity to practice, such as waiting for the bus in them morning – do so.

6 Having grasped the general idea, you can graduate to moving meditation. While walking you can focus on both your breaths and steps, working to coordinate the two into a harmonious rhythm. You might inhale for three steps and exhale for three steps – whatever works for you.

7 The Chi Kung exercises described in the next chapter represent a further evolution of the moving meditation concept. Focusing intently on slow, graceful, deliberate movements, coordinated with your breathing. Emphasise keeping your mind and body relaxed. Let yourself become absorbed with each part of every movement.

8 Moving meditation finds its full expression in Form and Mind Boxing discussed in the Chapter devoted to Stamina Training. This is an advanced form of practice when you have mastered the basic concepts of Calm Focus, Chi Kung and Stamina Training. Form and Mind Boxing is the ultimate synthesis of all the skills in this volume. The mental and physical effort required to coordinate mind and body will develop unparalleled focus here and now.

Variations

The examples given here meditative exercises to help you practise focusing here and now. None are inherently better than the others, merely different routes to the same goal. Equally none is expendable. Further, you can apply the general idea to any activity. Making breakfast, the walk to work and even using the photocopier would be just as good for practising mindful focus on the present.

Benefits

Once you've got hold of the general idea, learning to focus here and now will pay tremendous dividends. Most obviously, you'll be less distracted, able to concentrate more fully and get more out of everything you do. You'll probably find that once seemingly insoluble problems suddenly have a solution. A central reason for this is your mind won't be wandering of into the past or future. Meditative practice gives you the chance to relax, allowing your mental cogs to turn free from the interference of anxiety, worry and doubt. This turn makes you more likely to be happy now.

Calm Focus 2.8
Be kind, be careful, be yourself

Explanation

Eastern philosophy has an interesting tendency to seem a bit contradictory. Buddhism, for example, teaches that we can be happier if we focus here and now, and stop grasping after past and future. Having got hold of that idea it then goes on to say we should think very carefully about what we do now unless our past comes back to bite us later. This is generally referred to as Karma.

The central idea of Karma is fairly straightforward. If you're mean to someone now, they're more likely to be mean to you in the future, and you're probably going to suffer as a result. By carefully planting the seeds of good fortune now, we therefore avoid pain in the future. Karma is a funny thing, and this also means we're less likely to find ourselves grasping after some imperfect past further down the road.

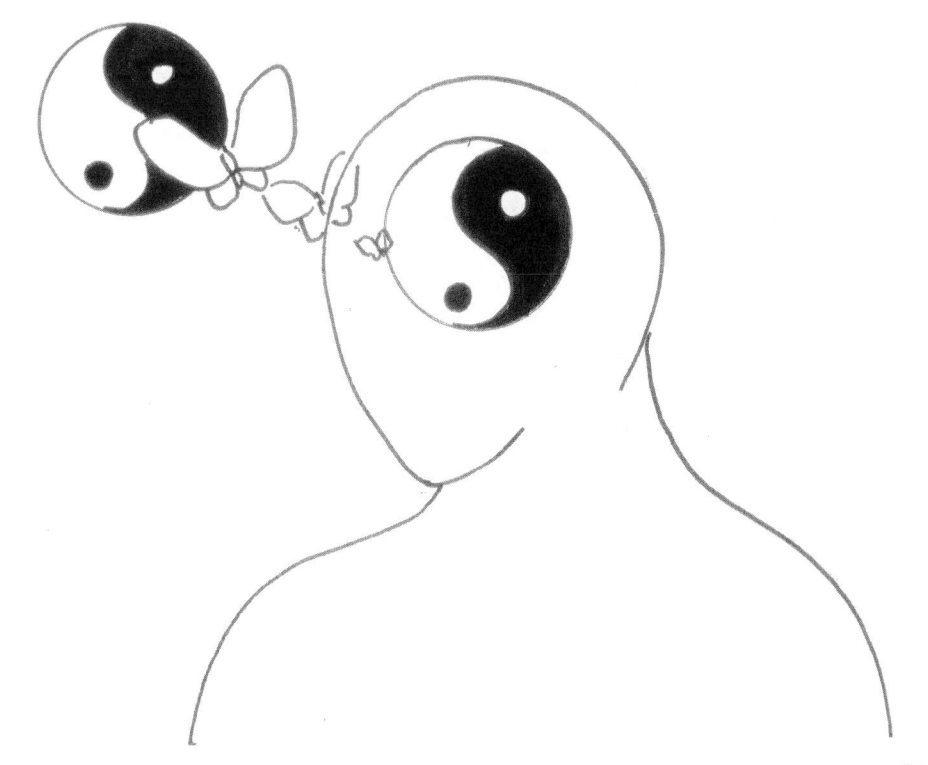

The famous Buddhist writer and philosopher Jack Korngold summarised going after good Karma quite simply as 'Be Kind, Be Careful, Be Yourself'. Essentially, this boils down to being mindful about how your actions now could affect you later. Without moralising, it's pretty obvious that deceit and deception are not solid foundations on which to build a future. Equally, you don't have to be a martyr to act with thoughtful integrity toward yourself and others, and while it may not always get you quite where you want to be, you can be happy when you get there.

Performance

1 Consider the last time you had a bad day. Perhaps work didn't go so well, you didn't reach a personal goal, or maybe the weather was just dull that day. Write down what it was for you.

2 Write a few words to express how you felt, such as 'bored, upset, frustrated, angry', or any combination that best describes how you felt.

3 Then, write a few words to describe any thoughts that you had at the same time. Such as 'I hate this job!', or 'I can't believe this weather, it's never going to improve' Whatever it was, write what best describes how you were thinking.

4 Now write a few words about how it made you act. Perhaps you were grumpy with someone, loafed at your desk counting the minutes before going home to pig out in front of the TV? How do you think this would affect the people around you? How did feeling and acting this way productively help you or anyone else?

5 Now take a moment to think over these last points. How could this come back to bite you later? For instance, perhaps being grumpy around the office will mean colleagues are less likely to help out with work. Equally, could work you haven't done now back up and create a problem in the future?

6 Re-read what happened, how you felt and how you acted. Try to rewrite your statements in a more positive and realistic way. If it helps, consider what your best friend would say to you to try and cheer you up. Then consider how this is likely to make you feel and act.

7 Write down how trying to see things more positively and realistically, and being mindful of its impact, could benefit you.

Variations

We touched on the butterfly effect at the outset of this chapter, and it's an appropriate place to close. Even your smallest actions can magnify to an enormous impact downstream. An offhand comment at the wrong time, for instance, could deliver a body blow to someone's confidence. Lack of confidence may be the only thing that prevents that person from attempting a difficult challenge that could have changed their life forever – or ours. It's a broad brushstroke example, but it illustrates the point. We can't bend the universe to our will, but by taking the time to consider your actions, we can at least set it spinning in the right direction.

Benefits

Remaining enigmatically contradictory, less is often more. It takes fewer muscles to smile than frown. It therefore takes less effort to exert a positive influence on ourselves and those around us. Our Karma is immeasurably improved by a little effort to be mindful of this fact.

Chapter 3

Chi Kung Training

Basic and advanced Chi Kung for stronger foundations

> "The purpose of life is to kindle a light in the darkness of mere being"
>
> Jung

Advanced Chi Kung 3.0
Advanced Chi Kung – developing a stronger foundation

What is Chi Kung?
Literally, Chi Kung means the art, or attainment, of energy. The practice of Chi Kung is older than recorded history, and probably developed in India before being brought to China sometime around 50 AD. Classical teaching has it that Chi (energy) circulates through the body, moving through pathways called meridians, and enables every function of life. Chi, which can also be translated as 'air', is believed to be accumulated from our surroundings, through specially developed breathing exercises. These focus on breathing using the abdomen, where Chi is believed to be stored. From there it is believed that mental focus can allow a practitioner to direct Chi anywhere in their body, such as to heal illness or protect their fist while breaking bricks. The practise of these exercises, or Chi Kung, has been used ever since to increase energy, promote physical health and mental wellbeing.

Energy and relaxation through Chi Kung
The Western jury is still out on the question of Chi, although the obvious health benefits to regular practitioners are compelling. The value of abdominal breathing, and Chi Kung in teaching us to do so, is, however, not in doubt. In the first instance, we know oxygen in the air we breathe fuels every activity of our lives. By the same token, your ability to fill your lungs with air limits everything you do. The lungs are inflated by expanding the rib cage and pushing the diaphragm (a sheet of muscle that separates your chest and tummy) down into the abdomen. The lungs are most effectively ventilated only when the diaphragm is used. Abdominal – Chi Kung – breathing allows you to take bigger breaths and bring more energy-giving oxygen on board.

On a higher lever, slow, deep breathing has an important effect on our heart and mental state. Breathing down into the abdomen impacts the flow of blood back to the heart, promoting a reduction in heart rate.

This in turn is fed back to the emotional centres of the brain to promote a sense of calm, relaxation and reduction in blood pressure. These effects are almost the reverse of the symptoms of mental anxiety. Chi Kung therefore allows you to regulate one of the most rapidly spreading epidemics of modern Western society, namely stress and anxiety. Finally, Chi Kung exercises gently stretch, mobilise and strengthen muscles and joints. This is therefore an ideal introduction to exercise, preparing the body for more demanding activity.

Advanced Chi Kung

Paradoxically, the slow, graceful movements of Chi Kung serve as an excellent foundation for very demanding physical activity. The ability to fill the lungs with oxygen is a vital link in the transfer of oxygen to working muscles. This is a central limitation to our stamina. Once delivered to the muscles, stamina is also limited by their ability to use oxygen. Larger, stronger muscle can consume more oxygen, generating greater power and physical performance. The Chi Kung postures stretch, strengthen and enhance the endurance of all the major muscle groups. Coordinating muscular activity is the final element of successful performance, prevented wasted effort and making the best of a limited supply of oxygen. Chi Kung training develops profound self-awareness and control, enhancing the rate at which skills can be acquired and dexterity with which they can ultimately be applied.

The Eight Pieces of Brocade is a Chi Kung set specifically developed to build a strong foundation of physical and mental readiness. According to legend, the set was created by Marshal Yue Fei, a senior officer in the Chinese Song Army around 1150AD. The Eight Pieces of Brocade was used in basic training of the Song soldiers, and to speed recovery after injury. The Eight Pieces of Brocade was also an essential primer to meet the demands of learning Eagle Claw Kung Fu, the creation of which Yue Fei is also credited. The set can be practices anywhere, has sufficient scope to remain challenging, and even has a version that can be practised while sitting. The Eight Pieces of Brocade has the virtue of being easy to learn while omitting none of the essential training objectives to build a strong foundation.

Benefits of Chi Kung

Chi Kung exercises can be performed almost anywhere and will provide several key benefits. These are:

- ◆ You will develop a greater sense of calm through Chi Kung training.
- ◆ The strength and mobility of muscles and joints will improve.
- ◆ This will have a positive impact on your blood pressure, heart and overall health.
- ◆ You will perform almost any physical activity to a higher level without becoming breathless.

Guidelines for Chi Kung training

- ◆ Keep an open mind. These exercises may seem unusual, but they work!
- ◆ Before beginning Chi Kung, clear your mind of all thoughts, especially negative ones.
- ◆ Take the time to master each exercise. There is no rush.
- ◆ The best time to practise is at the beginning or end of the day.
- ◆ Practise outside or in a clean air environment.
- ◆ Do not practise when you're in a hurry and cannot give it you full attention.

Using these exercises

These Chi Kung exercises are the most fundamental, and potentially valuable, of this entire volume. Their practise forms the foundation of everything that follows and I would recommend you work on them for at least a few weeks before moving on – you'll be glad you did! Each exercise forms the cornerstone of the next, building into a complete Chi Kung set. While you may eventually discard some movements, or perform them in a different order, make sure you have mastered performing the entire set first.

Chi Kung Training

Level White

Advanced Chi Kung 3.1
Abdominal breathing basics

Explanation

Oxygen fuels every activity of life. We exchange oxygen with the air through our lungs. The more fully we can inflate the lungs, the more efficiently we can get oxygen into our blood and then on to the tissues of our body. There are two principal elements to inflating the lungs, expanding the rib cage and chest, and pushing the diaphragm into the abdomen (tummy). To inflate the lungs fully we must use the diaphragm. As we do, the abdomen will be expanded. Similarly, to breath out fully, we must contract the abdomen. This simple Chi Kung exercise helps us learn to do so.

Performance

1 Stand in a relaxed posture; feet shoulder width apart.

2 Try to clear your mind or think about something positive.

3 Place the palm of your left hand on your tummy, about 5cm elow your navel. Place your right hand over your left.

4 Slowly breath in concentrating on breathing down into your abdomen. You'll feel your hands move outward slightly as you do. Be careful not to 'force' the process and don't actively try to push your tummy out; let the breathing do this.

5 When you've inhaled as far as you can, hold for two seconds.

6 Now begin to breathe out gently, and press gently with the palms of your hands. Keep going until you reach the end of the breath.

7 Hold for a second or two, release the pressure from your palms and begin breathing in. Do not maintain the pressure with your palms as you breathe in.

8 Continue for 9-10 breaths, then relax your arms to your side and breathe normally.

Variations

You can practise this exercise with your eyes closed if it helps. Focus specifically on the movement of your tummy felt through the palms of your hands. You may imagine the breath being light or golden as you breathe in, dark or black as you breathe out. Equally, you may imagine a light coming on as you breathe in and going out as you breathe out. These are all techniques to focus and calm the mind, focusing on something positive as you breathe in, so feel free to use whatever works for you.

Benefits

The ability to inflate the lungs properly will translate to easier breathing with almost any activity. As you become proficient, the rate at which you breathe will slow and depth will increase. People often tell you to take a deep breath when you're anxious. You may well notice yourself feeling calmer as a result of your practice.

Chi Kung Training

Level Yellow

Advanced Chi Kung 3.2
Small circulation,
Shen and the Bubbling Well

Explanation

Have you ever noticed how uncomfortable it feels when you're anxious or worried? That's probably why it is called being uptight. You feel tired, your muscles and limbs tense, and it's difficult to concentrate. Chinese medicine believes this is due to disrupted Chi flow in one of the major channels around the body.

As we breathe in, Chi is believed to flow down the front our body to a point just below the navel where it is stored – the Tantien. As we breathe out, it then moves up our back, over our head and back to our mouth. This so-called Small Circulation is driven by a combination of abdominal breathing and concentration. The circuit is completed by touching the tongue to the top of the mouth.

Anxiety prepares us for fight or flight, tensing the muscles and pulling them defensively in towards the body. You've probably felt the uncomfortable tension in the back of the neck when you've been worried, and felt relief from turning your head to stretch the muscles there. Chinese medicine believes tension in the neck constricts the small circulation, and that the 'Shen' (spirit or emotions) suffer the result of Chi stagnating there. Stretching the neck muscles is believed to restore Chi flow to the head, where the Shen resides, making us feel more positive.

From the Small Circulation, Chi is believed to flow out to the limbs, where it fuels all the processes of life. A smooth, steady flow is believed to be vital to good health. Many Chi Kung exercises are geared to building Chi and maintaining its movement around the body. A point on the base of the foot, called The Bubbling Well Cavity, is believed to be particularly important to driving Chi around the lower limbs. Whether you buy into the idea of Chi or not, you'll get more from the more advanced elements of your training if you build up a strong foundation. This first sequence of movements is designed to help promote relaxation and focus, along with some basic coordination between breathing and movement.

Performance

1 Stand in a relaxed posture, feet shoulder width apart, arms by your sides. Try to clear your mind or think about something positive. Touch your tongue to the top of your palate just behind your teeth.

2 Slowly inhale through your nose, concentrating on breathing down into your abdomen. As you breathe in, imagine your breath to flow down the front of your body to a point a few inches below your navel. If it helps, you can think of your breath as Chi, power energy or a bright light. You can imagine the spot just below your navel glowing as you breath down into it.

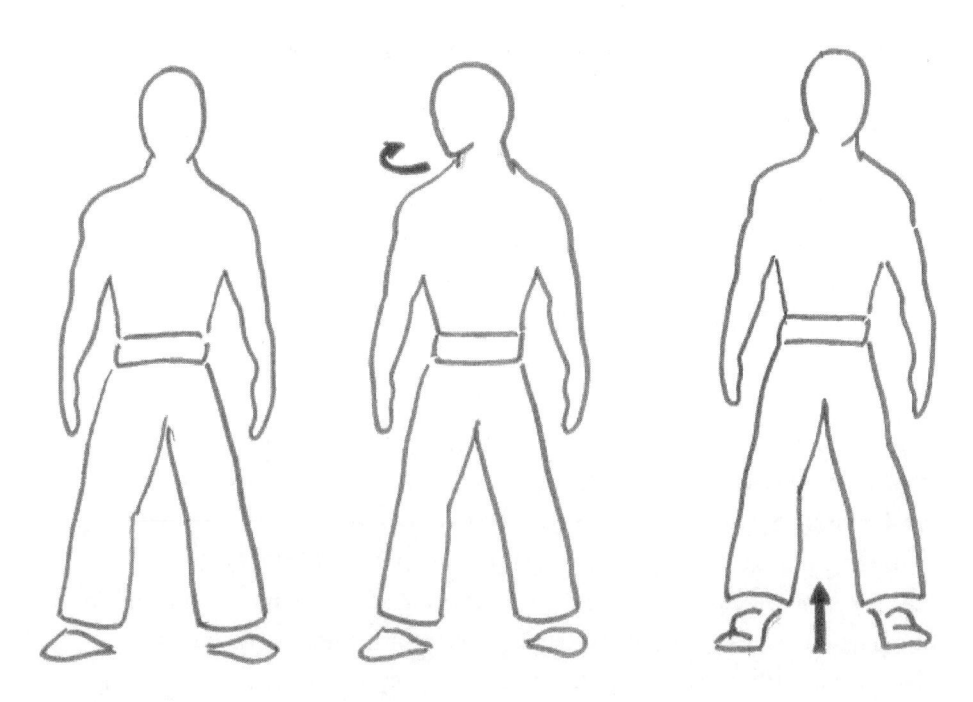

Chi Kung Training

3 As you breathe out, imagine this energy flowing through your groin, past your tailbone and up your spine. It passes over the top of your head, front of your face, and reaches the top of your mouth at the end of the breath.

4 When you've started to fall into a nice, relaxed rhythm with your breathing, begin to slowly turn your head to the side as you breathe in. Try to look back and, if it helps, imagine your troubles receding behind you. As you exhale, slowly turn your head to face front. Repeat to the other side. Continue turning your head from side to side until your neck muscles feel loose and relaxed. This is the First Piece of Brocade.

5 As you turn to face front for the last time, move without a break into the next movement. As you start to inhale, slowly raise yourself up on the ball of your foot. Pause for a moment at the top and then slowly lower yourself as you exhale. Bend your knees and drop your weight slightly at the bottom of the movement, then raise yourself up as you inhale. The movement should have a flowing, fluid quality to it as you raise and lower yourself in time with your breathing. Repeat the cycle until you feel completely calm, relaxed and focused. This is the Second Piece of Brocade

6 The transition between each form may feel a bit awkward at first. Concentrate on keeping your breathing deep and relaxed, and your movement speed slow. With practice you'll find a smooth, flowing transition from one movement to another – one that 'feels' right – will naturally evolve for you.

Variations

It is believed that adopting different arm positions will alter the flow of Chi. These movements can be practised with your hands by your sides, palms pressed against your lower back, or arms held out in front as if hugging a large ball. Each position has a different feel, so experiment and see what works for you. You can also use variations of these movements when sitting. A tense moment in the office can benefit from a few deep breaths and calm visualisation. A bit of a neck stretch makes a delayed train or bus a bit more bearable. Alternating pointing your toes with pulling them up toward your body loosens up stiff legs for particularly long spells of sitting.

Benefits

This opening sequence provides some useful exercises that will help you relax and focus your mind at any time. You'll also start to build coordination between breathing and movement, which you'll rely on for the more demanding exercises later on.

Advanced Chi Kung 3.3
The Triple Burner, original Jing and Lifting Palms

Explanation

When you're tired, you just can't beat a good stretch. After you've been stuck at your desk for hours, see how good it feels to lean back, stretch your arms out and take a long, deep breath. Chinese medicine attributes fatigue to stagnant Chi flow. This may occur when our posture constricts our breathing or the channels through which Chi is believed to pass. Stretching helps us breath more deeply and stretches the muscles through which the channel pass, supposedly opening them up. Whatever the explanation, it feels pretty good.

The second series of movements from The Eight Pieces of Brocade stretch the muscle of the upper body and especially the trunk. Traditionally, these movements are designed to encourage Chi flow through the Small Circulation and into the upper limbs. Stretching the arms upward expands the chest, facilitating deeper breathing. Bending forwards while exhaling compresses the midsection, mechanically supporting abdominal breathing.

Stretching the trunk forward and back is also believed to promote the health of the kidneys, the storehouse for original Jing (energy, or Chi you're born with), which facilitates further Chi accumulation. Stretching from side to side is thought to promote Chi flow through a second series of channels called the Triple Burner. These three channels circumvent the abdomen above the diaphragm, below the navel and at a point in between. They are associated with breathing, the spleen and digestion respectively.

Chinese and Western Medicine often seem to be at odds with each other, but at least one point on which they agree is the premium placed on the integrity of the lower back. The midsection is the pivot around which body turns, with the joint of the lower back carrying most of the load.

The muscles of the abdomen play an essential role in supporting the lower back. Enhancing lower back flexibility and the strength of the surrounding musculature, enormously reduces the incidence of debilitating back injury.

Performance

1 Stand in a relaxed posture, feet shoulder width apart, hands by your sides. Try to clear your mind or think about something positive. Take a deep breath into your abdomen.

2 Begin the first movement at the end of an exhalation. Begin to breathe in gently. Slowly draw your hands upward in front of your body so the palms are facing each other. Try and keep your hands and elbows as close to your body as you can.

3 Keep moving your hands upward. When your hands reach the level of your nose, interlink your fingers and clasp your hands together.

4 When your hands are over your head, turn your palms upwards while keeping your fingers interlinked. Straighten your arms and press your palms upward. Then slowly lean as far as you can to the left and right. As you straighten up, unlock your fingers and exhale as you lower your arms to your sides. Repeat five, seven or nine times, and then move straight on to the second movement.

Chi Kung Training

5 Begin the second movement at the end of an exhalation. Lift your fingers so your palms are facing the floor. Turn the fingers of each hand towards each other. Keep your elbows locked as you lift your hands in front of you and over your head. Look up at your hands as you stretch back.

6 As you begin to exhale, bring your arms down, keeping the elbows locked, and bend forward at the waist. Reach down toward the ground, grabbing your ankles or feet. Hold the position for a second or two before slowly returning the starting position. Repeat five, seven or nine times, and then move straight on to the third movement.

7 Begin the third exercise at the end of an exhalation, as you return to the starting posture of the second movement. As you breathe in, lift one arm overhead, as before, and press the other backward. Be sure to keep your shoulders square throughout. At the extreme range of motion, press upward and back forcefully. As you begin to exhale, start to raise the arm that was pushed back, while lowering the arm that was overhead. Keep your elbows locked. Your hands should pass somewhere around chest level at the end of an exhalation. Begin the second movement at the end of an exhalation. Repeat five, seven or nine times.

Variations

All of these movements can be practised while seated. You can do this in a chair (be careful if it's an office chair with casters!) or sitting on the floor with your legs stretched in front. If you feel a bit self-conscious, you can disguise the arm movements a little to suit your own level of modesty. While purists may argue against it, there is no need to be slavish to form. You should feel free to improvise if the mood, or desire not to attract attention, takes you. Pushing your palms forward, down and out to the side provide a good – and discreet – stretch to the muscles of the shoulder girdle.

Benefits

Chinese medicine suggests the health of the spine is critical to longevity. Whether the explanation is maintained Chi flow, or trunk muscles strong enough to prevent a crippling slipped disk, the foundation of core integrity will justify an investment of few minutes a day in your back. At a more mundane level, these movements are a Chi Kung set you can practise anywhere. Sitting at your desk, or on the red-eye to New York, this is the Chi equivalent of splashing cold water on your face.

Chi Kung Training

Level Red

Advanced Chi Kung 3.4
Heart Fire, Secret Sword & Drilling Fist

Explanation

If we are to continue improving, exercise must become progressively more demanding. This is true whether we're developing our muscles or our Chi. The final series of movements from The Eight Pieces of Brocade introduces postures that are physically more challenging than the previous set. These are combined with movements for the upper body aimed at helping us focus the mind more effectively on Chi development.

The Horse Stance is a staple of martial arts training. The wide foot spacing with thighs parallel to the floor places a huge demand on the muscles of the hip and thigh. Holding the body erect, particularly when we're simultaneously using our arms, also places tremendous emphasis on the muscles of the midsection. Working with this posture offers a remarkable challenge for the whole body even when little movement is involved. From the perspective of Chinese medicine, the Horse Stance is believed to have a potent effect on the kidneys, and the ability to accumulate Chi touched on in the previous section. This position is also believed to open the energy channels of the lower body, facilitating distribution of Chi to the legs.

We've already encountered the idea of releasing stagnant Chi from the first series of movements. There are several points around the body where stagnation is believed to occur, each of which is associated with a specific illness or malady. Accumulation of Chi at a spot close to the heart is associated with failure to expand the chest properly during breathing and produces – you guessed it – heartburn. Chi can also pool around the joints, when tense muscles are believed to compress and constrict flow through the energy channels.

The first series of movements is designed to expand the chest and loosen the muscles around the groin to facilitate Chi flow into the lower limbs. This not only promotes deeper breathing, relieving any heart fire, but also makes it considerably more comfortable to hold the Horse Stance for prolonged periods. The second movements further expand the chest, and also emphasize concentrated mental focus. It is believed this is essential to the accumulation and movement of Chi around the body. The final movement is designed to develop coordination between will, breath and action. This is a stepping-stone toward harmonious mastery of self, which stands at the heart of Chi Kung training.

Performance

1 Stand in a relaxed posture, feet shoulder width apart, arms by your sides. Take a deep breath into your abdomen. Try to clear your mind or think about something positive.

2 Place your feet about twice shoulder-width apart, toes pointing forward or slightly out. Keeping your back straight, sit back until your thighs are nearly parallel with the floor. Place your palms on your thighs, just above your knees, with the thumbs on the outside of your leg.

3 Take a deep breath. As you begin to exhale, turn your head to look back over your left shoulder. At the same time press your palms down on your thighs. Your right knee should dip toward the floor a little to accommodate the twisting motion. You should feel a gentle stretch across your chest and upper thighs. As you begin to inhale, return to the starting position. Repeat left and right alternately, five, seven or nine times as your condition improves.

4 Without pause, move straight on to the second movement. As you inhale, draw your hands up to the centre of your chest, palms facing together. As you palms reach chest height, slowly turn your head to look left.

5 The arm action is now just like drawing a longbow. Form a fist with your right hand and forcefully pull the elbow back as if pulling the bowstring. You should feel a satisfying stretch across your chest and shoulders, as well as tension in your upper back. At the same time, slowly and purposefully, drive the left hand forward, pointing with the first two fingers. Concentrate all your attention on the hand pointing forward, called The Secret Sword. As you inhale, bring your hand back in from of your chest, with palms open and facing each other. Repeat left and right alternately, five, seven or nine times as your condition improves.

6 When you reach the end of the second sequence, inhale and draw your fists down to your sides, elbows back. As you begin to exhale, look to your left, glaring fiercely at an imaginary opponent. Now, slow and purposefully drive your left fist out to your left side. Focus all your attention on this Drilling Fist. Imagine power rushing down your arm and into the fist.

7 As you fully extend your left arm, clench the fist tightly. At the same time pull the elbow of the opposite arm back forcefully and clench the fist. Imagine your Drilling Fist is driven by unstoppable power, crashing into and through your opponent.

8 As you begin to inhale, draw your left fist back to your side and look forwards. Repeat left and right alternately, five, seven and nine times as your condition improves.

Variations

There is no getting away from the fact the Horse Stance is tough. So, if it's too much to start with, or you just feel you can't, start with a stance which is somewhere between normal standing and the full-blown Horse. Work 'down' to the full Horse Stance gradually by keeping to the same number of repetitions of each exercise, but dropping a little lower each time you practise. While it might not seem like it on your first attempt, you'll soon be able to hold the Horse for minutes at a time. You can also perform versions of these movements while sitting. Looking back over your shoulder while keeping your hands on your knees is particularly good for relieving a stiff back induced by hours hunched over your desk.

Benefits

The Horse Stance develops tremendous power in the lower limbs. You'll soon notice how attention to Horses carries you more easily up stairs, accompanied by a blistering increase in your time over ten furlongs. The Secret Sword and Drilling Fist have a meditative quality whose benefits will be felt through improved sense of self-awareness, calm and well being. These exercises also introduce the basic coordination of will, breath and action, which serves as a basis for the more demanding training detailed in later chapters.

Chi Kung Training

Level Blue

Advanced Chi Kung 3.5
The Eight Pieces of Brocade

Explanation

When you have mastered each section of The Eight Pieces of Brocade, you can build them into one continuous Chi Kung Set. The integration of all three sections increases the physical and mental challenge of your Chi Kung training, building a strong foundation for the more demanding exercises detailed later.

The object of the set is to systematically prepare the mind and body for intense physical activity. All of the major joints are mobilised while strengthening the muscles that support them. Many of the movements are geared toward encouraging deeper breathing and coordinating this with our movements. Both enhance the supply of oxygen to the working muscles, helping us resist fatigue.

These harmonising effects are ultimately achieved through mental concentration directed toward each movement of the set. The intense focus on each form helps us exclude distraction, build calm, self-awareness and the profound single-mindedness of purpose that is central to meeting any challenge life has to offer.

Performance

1 Open the first section of The Eight Pieces of Brocade. Perform each movement slowly and deliberately. When you reach the end of the first section, go straight into the second and then third part of the set without a break.

2 To begin with, just perform a few repetitions of each movement before making a slow, smooth transition to the next form. The third part of the set is more demanding than the preceding parts, and you might not be able to finish if you go in with too many repetitions at the outset. Build the number of repetitions up gradually as your condition improves.

3 You may find that your breathing becomes a little irregular or poorly coordinated with your movements. You may also have trouble remembering each move when you have to string them all together for the first time. This is a quite normal consequence of concentration and natural desire to perform the set well. Remember, there is no finish line and no rush. Simply slow down, focus intently on your breathing and take your time.

4 Once you've mastered the sequence, start working on coordinating your breathing with each movement. After a little practice you should notice each movement naturally ebbs and flows with each breath. The same will be true of the transitions between each form.

5 As breathing and movement become automatically synchronised, focus more on the feeling of each movement. If it helps, look directly at the limbs that are in action and try to imagine the inner workings that are keeping them moving.

6 In the final stage, visualise Chi, power, or whatever you want to call it, filling your body with each breath. Try to think of yourself becoming more vital and powerful with each breath. Use your mental focus to drive this Chi into the moving of your limbs as you exhale, making them increasingly powerful and strong with each breath.

7 Close the set by returning to a relaxed standing position and practicing some slow, abdominal breathing. Close your eyes if it helps. Take a moment to enjoy a sense of calm relaxation before ending the set.

Variations

You don't have to practise the set in this order, and it is presented here to in a logical order of increasing exercise intensity. Several versions of The Eight Pieces of Brocade can be found in original texts with different ordering. Chi Kung purists may want to look these up, while pragmatist may eventually omit all but the forms they feel serve them best.

Benefits

The Eight Pieces of Brocade is a relatively simple Chi Kung set. It rewards us with the building blocks of a higher state of physical readiness and calm focus. Practising the entire Eight Pieces of Brocade with growing repetitions offers a structure within which to develop foundations for the more improvised Form and Mind Boxing detailed in the following chapter. The combination of basic skills and enhanced conditioning acquired here are in turn central to the practice of Hard Kung exercises detailed in the chapter on Developing Power.

Level Black

Advanced Chi Kung 3.6
Cutting cloth to suit your means

Explanation

When we become totally engrossed in something we enjoy, time seems to stand still; we become calm, focused and happy. These moments often precipitate great insights, where seemingly insoluble problems suddenly become clear. Chi Kung is a vehicle through which to achieve this state of harmony between body and mind. Ultimately the objective it aims to reach is tranquillity and insight.

The patterned movements of Chi Kung sets were developed to strengthen physical constitution and facilitate our ability to focus on this higher objective. Through undivided attention on a series of physical movements, we forget trivial worries and daily concerns, allowing the mind to grow quiet. Through regular practice we more easily recognise and acquire this tranquil state, where it is traditionally believed we are open to insights of higher wisdom.

Beyond basic conditioning, The Eight Pieces Of Brocade set offers a convenient structure within which to develop a harmonious state. The specific movements themselves are not essential. There is no reason at all that your walk to the office, housework or physical exercise cannot become Chi Kung. The basic principles can be applied anywhere and to anything.

Performance

1 The simplest activity you can transform into Chi Kung is probably walking. It's convenient, can be practised anywhere and allows you to practise Chi Kung discreetly.

2 Start by becoming mindful of the walking action and movement of the lower limbs. These have become so automatic for most of us that we never give them any thought

3 Walking at normal speed, concentrate on slow, deep abdominal breaths. Try to bring your striding rhythm into synch with your breathing; say, one breath for every 10 steps, whatever works for you.

4 Once you've got it into a steady rhythm, shift your focus to the details of each step. This can be anything that catches your attention. You may choose to focus on the sensation in your foot as it strikes the floor, or the swing through the knee as you stride out.

5 Now focus on your breathing again, imagining Chi, power or energy flowing into you with each breath. As you breathe out, visualise Chi flowing to your lower limbs, driving the movements you're focused on.

6 Your practice will develop a state of intense concentration, which may well shut out a big chunk of the world. The assault on your senses can be a little disorientating when your focus suddenly swings wide open again. So, when you're ready to stop practising, take a moment or two to come down. Stand still for a moment, take stock of any insights from your practice, and then move on.

Variations

Having grasped the basic principles, you can transform any activity into Chi Kung. As with The Eight Pieces of Brocade, begin practicing with simple tasks and movements at first. Practice slowly and in short bursts at first, working up to more vigorous and extended practice as your concentration grows. It's also easier to break down more complex activities into their component parts, practicing each separately, before applying Chi Kung to the whole task. You can eventually apply these ideas to your stamina training using the Form and Mind Boxing discussed in the next chapter.

Benefits

The ability to give concentrated attention to any action or event is a powerful skill. You will find it easier to pick up new skills or apply those you have. With everything you do, heightened awareness will help you get more out of it. This may manifest itself as heightened insight, wisdom, or simple pleasure.

Chapter 4

Stamina Training

Basic and advanced Kung Fu exercises for endurance and weight control

"Between us and excellence, the gods have placed the sweat of our brows"

Hesiod

Stamina training 4.0
Stamina – Basic and Advanced Kung Fu exercises for endurance and weight control

How stamina training works

Whenever we want to lift or move something, we have to produce the force to do so from our muscles. This process requires energy, and the more muscle we use at one time, the more energy we require. The fuel to drive our muscles comes from the food we eat and the oxygen we breathe in. Muscles have enough fuel built in for short burst of work, but to continue for longer periods they must be supplied by additional resources from the blood, pumped by the heart. Once again, the more muscle we use, the more energy we require and the harder the heart must work to provide oxygen. Equally, the harder we must breathe.

> Stamina training helps us increase our readiness to perform longer bouts of work, exercise or play. There are three vital links in this process:
> - Breathing properly, to get the maximum amount of air and oxygen into the lungs.
> - Training the heart to deliver oxygen-rich blood to the muscle.
> - Training the muscles to be able to use more oxygen when it is delivered.

Combined arm and leg stamina training

Clearly, the best way to train for stamina is to use as many muscles as possible at one time, for prolonged periods. The most effective way to accomplish this aim is to exercise our arms and legs at the same time. Combined arm and leg exercise produces the greatest overall workload, and therefore training for the heart and breathing. Equally, as many muscles as possible are trained to use more oxygen. This is the basis for Kung Fu stamina training.

Advanced training principles

Many activities aimed at developing stamina rely on stereotyped movement patterns whose energetic efficiency means they can be carried on for long periods without fatigue. Marathon races can only be completed because participants have learned to be co-ordinated and extremely efficient, conserving energy to minimize the demands on their heart, lungs and muscles. We can deliberately reduce efficiency, and enhance conditioning potential, by countering the effects of improved co-ordination. In the context of stamina training, there are several ways we can accomplish this objective.

Few of us can move our legs with the finesse or speed to match our arms. Bringing the legs up to speed offers tremendous potential to increase workloads. Faster movements become progressively less efficient, particularly when fatigue impacts our coordination. Working at unusually high rates, such as in sprinting or interval training, demands a quantum leap in energy output. A further step is to deliberately use movements that place the limbs at a mechanical disadvantage, therefore increasing the load carried by our muscles. You can feel this effect by walking in a slight crouch compared with standing up straight. Finally, we can compensate for improved coordination by making the muscles work against a greater load. Punching while carrying a small dumb-bell demands a proportionate increase in work for the same speed and range of movement.

> ### Benefits of stamina training
> Stamina training has been shown to deliver a number of valuable benefits. Most important are:
>
> ◆ The heart becomes stronger and less liable to disease, especially coronary artery disease.
>
> ◆ The chemistry of the blood changes to further reduce the chance of heart disease, mainly by lowering cholesterol, which contributes to coronary artery disease.
>
> ◆ Blood pressure (associated with 50% of all deaths when elevated) tends to reduce.
>
> ◆ We become more able to sustain heavy exercise. Previously difficult activities feel easier.
>
> ◆ Our resistance to fatigue goes up, we have more energy and recover quickly when tired.
>
> ◆ The high levels of energy expenditure (highest during combined arm and leg exercise), helps weight control.

Using these exercises

These exercises will systematically develop your stamina. Each exercise builds the foundation for the next. Be sure to work through the exercises in order, progressing to the next level only when you have mastered the previous one. There is no rush and you will not get the most from your training if you neglect getting the basic foundations right. Patience and diligent practice will reward you with much better and more sustainable results.

This chapter starts with a review of the basic kicking, punching and moving techniques of the Wing Chun stamina training method. We then move on to examine movement patterns deliberately designed to reduce your efficiency, enhance your power output and training effects. Techniques are illustrated to train the upper and lower limbs progressively. Finally, two alternative training methods are illustrated, based on soft and hard styles of Kung Fu.

Stamina Training

Guidelines for stamina training

There are no hard and fast rules, but here are some pointers on stamina training:

- Train no less than an hour after eating or an hour before doing so.
- Drink plenty of water and keep hydrated.
- Do not exercise if you have drunk alcohol beforehand and refrain from smoking.
- A specific warm up is probably not required, but start at around 50% of your top effort and build up the effort over a few minutes.
- Work at a level which makes you breathe hard, but where you're not fighting for breath.
- Work continuously and rhythmically in any stamina exercise.
- Throw in bursts of intense effort every now and again to really push yourself.
- Train at this pace for 20-30 minutes 4-5 times a week.
- Focus on combined arm and leg exercises, and specifically using large muscle groups like the shoulder girdle, back and legs.
- Train for stamina before you train for strength, as power training will tire you out
- Ease down from maximum effort; don't just stop.

Masters Mind and Body: Advanced Kung Fu techniques for personal transformation

Level White

Stamina Training 4.1
Stance, punching and stepping basics

Explanation

The Character Two stance is named after the Chinese character that its shape resembles. This is the basic training stance of Wing Chun Kung Fu and the foundation of the fighting stance we use in moving and kicking. The chain punch is used to attack an opponent with a flurry of strikes that are very difficult to defend. This technique utilises muscles from the entire upper body and is a very demanding exercise. Chasing steps bring the legs into the equations, allowing us to move the whole body weight while punching. The combination of arm and leg work forms the basis of Wing Chun stamina exercise.

Performance

1 To open the Character Two stance, start with your feet together, hands by your sides. Bend your knees slightly, dropping your body about 10cm. Keeping your heels in place, turn your feet outward about 45 degrees. Now keep the balls of your feet in place and turn your heels outward so your feet end up pointing inward about 45 degrees. Push your backside forward and your knees together so there is about one fist distance between them. Your legs and buttocks should be tensed.

2 To chain punch, start by place your left hand, palm in and fingers pointing upward, about 10cm from the centre of your chest. Place your right hand, palm in and fingers pointing

forward, reaching forward so the elbow is alongside the left hand. Form your hands into a fist with the knuckles aligned vertically and the thumb on top of the hand. With the rear hand, punch down the centre line of the body at nose level. At the same time withdraw the other hand toward the chest under the punch. You'll finish in an on-guard position with hands the other way around.

3 Chasing steps are made from the fighting or on guard stance. From the Character Two stance, keep your heels in place and turn the toes of the right foot outward so your feet are parallel. Turn to the right and shift 70-80% of your weight onto your back leg. Step forward with your right leg, dragging the rear foot up behind it while keeping it in contact with the ground. Keep punching as you step.

Variations

Practise opening and closing the stances ten times or more in succession. Practise holding the stance for a minute or more, keeping your legs tensed and breathing steady as you do. Practise launching a series of punches at different heights. Try cycling the hands in the reverse direction. The rear hand comes forward, under the lead arm as you pull it back.

Benefits

Few exercises target the upper body for stamina training and even fewer will tax them like chain punching. Equally, you'll quickly find practising this stance toning up your thighs and backside.

Masters Mind and Body: Advanced Kung Fu techniques for personal transformation

Level White

Stamina Training 4.2
Turning, kicking and boxing basics

Explanation

If you keep punching and stepping, eventually you're going to bump into a wall. This exercise shows us how to turn from the Character Two stance. Once we've coordinated the arms and steps in attack and movement, we bring in the big guns with kicking. Kicking, punching and stepping are the bread-and-butter of Wing Chun stamina training. The conditioning potential of all four limbs working together outstrips almost every other stamina exercise. Mastering these skills provides a firm platform for the more advanced conditioning techniques discussed later.

Performance

1 Open the Character Two stance and turn to form the on guard position facing to your right. To turn to face the direction you've come from, turn the lead foot inward so the heel is facing forward. You'll feel some tension in your hips trying to turn you as you do. Keeping the lead foot firmly planted on the ground, turn to the rear swinging your lead arm out and around forcefully. Then snap your arms into the on guard as if facing an opponent stalking you from behind. As you turn, let the toes of the left foot turn out so the feet are parallel. Drop your weight back over the rear leg and you've completed an about-face.

2 Wing Chun kicks are driven from the hip and followed by a step. Before you step, drive the leading foot up from the ground in a

kick to an imaginary opponent's shin. Rather than returning the kicking foot to its original position, let it fall forward, about the distance of a natural step. Drag the back foot up towards the lead foot. Work these kicks in with your stepping and keep chain punching as you go.

3 Gradually work up to 'boxing' for three to five-minute rounds, with a minute of rest in between. Increase intensity by extending each 'round', adding more, reducing rest periods, or all of these together. Aim for a total work time of 20-30 minutes, including rest periods, three to five times a week. Throw in bursts of all-out effort every now and again to really push yourself.

Variations

Add a series of chain punches before you turn and when you reach the final position of the turn. Imagine you are facing and taking out multiple opponents. As you turn try to swing your arm out in a chopping motion before assuming the on guard. This will increase the workload on the waist muscle. Try driving kicks to shin, knee, and waist level and higher as your flexibility improves. When you kick forward, try holding the kicking leg outstretched for a few seconds and chain punch before you set the foot down.

Benefits

Punching, stepping and kicking offers unsurpassed exercise for the entire body. Even the muscles of the abdomen will be called forcefully into play as you lift your legs to kick and turn your body. Once you've mastered these techniques, and can keep going for extended periods, you will have a tool to promote an unprecedented level of conditioning – and it can all be done in a space no bigger than your living room!

Stamina Training 4.3
Splitting hands

Explanation

Wing Chun Kung Fu contains three empty hand sets. The third form is variously called 'The Moon Pointing Finger' or 'Form of Desperation'. The idea is broadly that no matter how good you are, it's the nature of fighting to go horribly wrong. An unexpectedly fierce opponent could push you badly out of position; you may have to think outside the box to avoid being overwhelmed. The splitting hands technique is used to present a massive defensive area, slipping around or deflecting an opponent while you regroup for another assault. Combined with stepping footwork, the exaggerated arm movements offer a real challenge for both the musculature of the upper body and stabilising muscles of the waist.

Stamina Training

Performance

1 Start in the on guard position with your left hand and left leg forward.

2 The splitting hands involves both arms acting together. Keeping the left hand at eye level, the forearm is driven across the chest. The right hand is driven in an arc down across the tummy.

3 The elbow of the left arm will end up alongside the elbow of the right arm, effectively forming a bar down the right side of the body.

4 To switch sides, the left hands arcs down and across the body, inside the right forearm. The right hand is driven up and across the body keeping the elbow on the same level throughout.

5 A slight twist of the waist in the direction of the deflection adds power to the whole movement.

6 The movement is finished off when combined with a step backwards. Holding in mind that the idea is to avoid a powerful opponent, this retreating moves you back, to the side and hopefully out of the way of the enemy onslaught. The step is made by driving the leg backwards and to the side on the opposite side to the deflection.

7 Repeat the retreating step on the opposite side as you change hands from one side to the other.

Variations

When you arrive in the final position of the splitting deflection, simply drive the whole shape across to the other side of the body with a powerful snap of the waist and a step forward. You can imagine that your splitting hand may have caught an opponent's incoming limb and you are simply driving it out of the way. You can also use the splitting hands to cover yourself as you turn. Once you've completed your defensive moves, try driving a strike or push from either hand before resuming chain punches.

Benefits

Quite aside from the introduction of retreating steps, this technique offers an interesting range of challenges for your co-ordination, not to mention upper body stamina and power.

Stamina Training 4.4
Double punch

Explanation

Chain punches are the workhorses of Wing Chun. Their power relies on a rapid volley of strikes driven forward into the opponent. Faced with a sudden attack from the side, we may not have time to set up a guard or even be in the right position to use it. The double punch can be used to launch a power assault to the side, whether your standing still or changing direction from a flurry of chain punches. The exaggerated arm movement and sudden turn provide a thorough challenge for the shoulder girdle and waist.

Performance

1 To begin with, practise this movement from a relaxed standing or Character Two stance.

2 Imagine you see an opponent to your left. As you turn to meet them the left hand is flung out at head level. You attempt to hit them with the back of your hand.

3 You continue to turn toward your opponent, drawing the left hand down toward your left side.

4 The right hand now throws a haymaker or hook at head level. The right fist will end up somewhere beyond your left shoulder.

5 Repeat the process on the opposite side until you can perform it smoothly.

6 Join up the movements by starting the turn to one side from the final position of the previous punches. You'll find your fist performing a massive figure eight across the front of your body.

7 Finally, try the movement while stepping forward and backward. This will not only increase the overall workload, but also place a very noticeable extra demand on the postural muscle of your waist.

8 When you put more power into the double punch you'll find the moment will make your waist twist further and give a tendency

to lean over the knee of the lead leg. Considered very bad form in fighting, because it wastes energy and put you off balance, the lack of efficiency is ideal for driving up the workload in stamina training.

Variations

Increasing the rate of punches will emphasize the muscles of the waist and shoulder. Alternatively you can exaggerate the range of motion in the arm movement, wait, twist, bend to the side or accompanying knee bend. In its ultimate evolution, use the double punch as you turn and change direction. For those with an active imagination, add a ducking motion at the end of the movement, as if your punches have missed and you're ducking the retaliation.

Benefits

This combination has tremendous room for growth and increasing workload. The fully evolved double punch offers an extremely high level of control. You can benefit from thorough conditioning for almost every muscle group in your body, or take the opportunity to concentrate your effort on a specific area if you wish.

Stamina Training 4.5
Dragon Steps

Explanation

Legend has it that the techniques of Shaolin Kung Fu evolved from observation of animal movements. Imitating a particular animal was associated with improvement in a specific facet of fighting and health. The tiger forms, for instance, are associated with increased muscle strength and powerful striking ability. The leopard is similarly associated with speed and grace. As most of us cannot claim to have seen a dragon, the origins of this form are a little hazier. The dragon is venerated in China as the embodiment of good fortune and strength. The forms are probably an attempt to interpret artistic representations of the period. Associated with solid bones and stance, the Dragon Step probably represents the coils of its body. Dragon Steps are a powerful tool for shaping grace, posture and the muscles of the entire lower body.

Performance

1 Start in the on guard position with your left hand and left leg forward.

2 Step forward with the rear leg, pointing the toes of the right foot outward. Your shoulders and body will twist slightly toward the right.

3 The right foot passes in front and slightly across the left foot. Toes point outward at about 45 degrees and your knees are close together.

4 Taking your weight on the left leg, drop into a slight crouch and place the right foot on the floor. You'll find yourself leaning forward slightly to keep your balance.

5 Crouch as low as possible, supporting your weight on the left leg.

6 Now shift your weight to the leading, right leg and stand up. Repeat on the opposite side.

7 When you've got the hang of it, the sequence will see you tangle and untangle your lower limbs with your body gracefully rising and falling with each step.

8 Begin by splicing a couple of Dragon Steps into a segment of steady boxing. Make your Dragon Stepping intervals longer as your condition improves.

Variations

You can alternate steps on the right and left leg, or perform a sequence on one side – both are good. Try throwing a kick from the rear foot as you stand up. You can also co-ordinate stepping with your hand movements. Try pressing your palms down following the movement in the first stage of the step, driving a punch forward as you rise up.

Benefits

Dragon Steps make a novel departure from the bread-and-butter stamina moves. Few exercises can claim to provide such a complete challenge for postural stability, flexibility, stamina and coordination.

> Level Red

Stamina Training 4.6
Crouching Tiger

Explanation

There are many forms of Kung Fu. Some almost exclusively emphasize hand strikes, while others include a variety of kicks. Crouching Tiger is a basic training exercise that aims to strengthen the kicking muscles of the hips and thigh, while also promoting greater flexibility. Overcoming gravity in a vertical jump requires a huge amount of effort from the most powerful muscle of the body. The energy demands in this type of activity are almost unparalleled by any other exercise. As your first experience with show you, Crouching Tiger is an excellent way to shift your exercise workload and conditioning up a notch or two.

Performance

1 Beginning from the on guard position, crouch down. Place your left hand on the floor in front of your left foot.

2 Push your right leg out to the side. Hold you right arm straight out to the side, level with the floor. This is the starting position for crouching tiger.

3 Jump upward, driving off the floor with the left leg.

4 As you become airborne, draw the right knee up toward the chest and reach up as high as you can with the right hand.

5 Land on two feet, bending your knees to absorb the landing force and dropping back down into the crouching position.

6 Repeat on the opposite side.

7 Throw Crouching Tiger into your stamina work as and when you feel the urge, or want to ramp up the workload. Start with single repetitions built into steady work and gradual add repetitions, increasing your Crouching Tiger intervals, as your condition improves.

Variations

It's useful to couple this movement with a healthy imagination. Use the initial crouch to avoid a high strike, jumping to evade a sweep or low kick. You can increase the intensity of this exercise by crouching lower at the start, attempting to jump higher and driving the knee lift higher. As your condition improves, you can also try landing on just one leg. If you find don't want the complication of the fully-fledged movement, or simply don't feel you can, start off with a straightforward vertical jump. This is already an excellent addition to your arsenal of stamina-enhancing techniques. The tuck jump, where you pull the knees to the chest in flight, is a good halfway house to Crouching Tiger.

Benefits

The muscles of the hip and thigh are the most powerful of the human body. They are specifically emphasized in jumping and Crouching Tiger. You'll soon notice a significant increase in overall stamina and explosive power throughout the lower body. There's also a payoff for flexibility with a thorough stretch for the groin, back and hips.

Stamina Training 4.7
Flying and triple kicks

Explanation

We will not meet all opponents eye to eye. They may be considerably bigger, have the advantage of high ground, or in days gone by been mounted on horseback. Jumping kicks evolved to even the odds with a taller assailant. They also provided for highly impressive, acrobatic demonstrations when Kung Fu bodyguards found themselves unemployed and in need of additional income.

An opponent may not only be bigger, they may also be stronger and heavier than us. As a counter to greater power Kung Fu uses legendary speed. The triple kick aims to deliver several strikes to the opponent's one, creating greater cumulative damage. In normal kicking, a great deal of the power is generated from the thrust of the supporting leg. During the triple kick the lead foot never touches the ground, forcing the hips and thighs to work extremely hard; a feature that makes this technique a particularly good exercise.

Performance

1 Start from the on guard position with the left foot forward and weight on your rear leg. Shift your weight forward onto your left leg, as if taking a step forward, and use the momentum to jump upward from the left foot. Keep your hands in the on guard position with the elbows tucked in. Try to avoid letting your arms flail about, as this can unbalance you.

2 As you jump, lift the knee of the right leg as high as possible. As soon as you feel the knee has gone as high as possible, drive the right leg down toward the floor. You'll feel the reaction trying to drive the left leg forward. Go with it, launching a kick to the front. You touch down on the right foot, with the left leg landing in front back in the on guard position.

3 Keep kicks low to start, aiming for an imaginary opponent's knee or groin. As you feel more comfortable cautiously aim for higher target. When you've really got to grips with it, try launching a medley of kicks, one after the other. This can be from one leg, or alternating.

4 The triple kick is simpler to describe than perform. Starting from the on guard position kick forward. Then, without putting the foot on the floor, drive another two kicks forward using the muscles of the thighs and hips before placing your foot back down.

5 Once again, keep the kicks low to start with and build height gradually. Once mastered, try increasing the number of kicks you can place before putting your foot down.

Variations

The jumping kick is tricky if you've never tried it before. To make things simpler, it can be broken into two phases. Begin by simply taking the step forward, jump and raise your knee. Add the kick once you've landed. Gradually speed things up. As your speed increases you'll naturally find the two elements knitting together. Advanced practitioners can also benefit from breaking up this flying kick. Putting more aggression into the knee lift makes it a strike. The technique is rounded out by reaching forward and pulling an imaginary opponent into the oncoming knee.

Benefits

Few of us attempt to use our legs as we would our arms. Jumping and triple kicks massively increase the potential workload carried by the lower limbs. Once mastered, you can elect to shift the emphasis of your stamina work up and down your body at will. With the combination of fast kicks and fast punches, your workloads will spiral upward tremendously.

Stamina Training 4.8
Form and Mind Boxing

Explanation

The Chinese martial arts are broadly broken down into soft and hard forms. Kung Fu is generally regarded as a hard, or external martial art, focused on training to develop powerful strikes and kicks. The soft martial arts include Tai Chi, Ba Kua and Hsing-I, whose forms and patterns aim to nurture internal harmony and health. Ba Kua and Hsing-I are less familiar to westerners than Tai Chi, but share the emphasis on relaxed, graceful movement. Ba Kua involves walking in continuous tight circle or figure eight, flowing from movement to movement while integrating breath and mind. The practice of so-called Form and Mind Boxing draws together all of the previous lessons, integrating Chi Kung, calm focus and stamina exercises. The open-ended nature of Form and Mind lends itself to stamina training while adding a meditative quality to your practice.

Performance

1 Begin Form and Mind practice when you can comfortably chain punch, step and kick for several 3-5 minute rounds.

2 Find a space where you can map out a circle about 8 feet across, either in your mind or actually drawn on the floor. Stand on one edge of the circle and practice a few deep breaths while clearing your mind. Open the Character Two stance and assume the on guard position.

3 Begin chain punches, steps and kicks around your circle. Take things fairly slowly at first, about half your normal speed. Concentrate on keeping your movements relaxed and fluid. Focus on your slow, deep breaths, down into you abdomen. If thoughts enter your mind, acknowledge them and let them go, bringing your focus back to walking the circle.

4 When you have walked the circle a few times, change directions and go back on your self. Turn using the swinging arm, splitting

hands, double punch, a kick or simply moving your guard around to face the other way. Try different combinations. Keep punching, stepping and kicking without pause once you've changed direction. Focus on continuous movement.

5 Once you've got the hang of walking the circle, change direction as and when you feel like it. Imagine you are fighting opponents coming in from all angles, whirling around to meet each new attack. This may be after a few steps, or walking in one direction for many circuits. Also, try a few steps backwards using the splitting hands and retreating steps.

6 Gradually speed up, but not at the expense of losing your focus. Keep your breaths slow and deep, your mind clear, your movements fluid and continuous. You can stay working with boxing rounds, or go for prolonged periods as a slower pace as the spirit moves you.

7 For variety, try walking a figure eight within the same size circle. This has a slightly different feel about it as it involves tighter turns. For a real challenge try walking a series of two figure eights together, either one on top of the other or in a line, but all in the same 8-foot boundary.

Variations

Coupled with a healthy imagination you can really let yourself go on this one. The sudden twists and turns lend Form and Mind Boxing a dynamic and highly charged quality that is more exuberant than basic chain punch, step and kick. The addition of music adds to the dance-like quality, shifting the psychological focus from exercise to something more fun. Feel free to improvise martial techniques as they feel appropriate to you, or copy those you've seen on TV. No one is expecting you to demonstrate refined technical prowess, but most of us can deploy a fairly convincing chop to the side of an opponent's neck, or throw a few martial shapes to music. Within the basic boundaries, remaining focused on mind, breath and continuous relaxed movement, improvisation adds interest and fun. As a variation to chasing steps, you can try using the traditional Ba Kua footwork. To do this, simply assume a slight crouch and step one foot in front of the other keeping the knees close together at all times. For those with a more spiritual bent, a useful meditative practice is to imagine breathing Chi to your lower abdomen as you inhale, using your mind to help it flow out to your limbs with each exhalation. Once again, the right choice of music really lubricates the cosmic wheels here.

Benefits

Borrowing heavily from the soft arts, Form and Mind is the ultimate synthesis of Kung Fu stamina training, integrating the skills of mind, breath and movement in one complete practice.

Stamina Training 4.9
The Way of the Warrior

Explanation

The Samurai are probably the most famous martial export of Japan. Their code of conduct, Bushido, encapsulates the unending struggle for self-improvement and mastery of self. Physical and mental exercises are routes through which these ideas can still find expression in modern life. They present the opportunity to challenge preconceived (and often self-imposed) limitations, refine our abilities and increase self-knowledge. Further, the attitude of positive self-improvement nurtures a willingness to accept not only that new ideas may be valid, but also that previously sacred facts may be in error. For instance, common wisdom has it that the best way to improve stamina and lose body fat is to exercise at a steady, unbroken pace – this is not so. The Tabata Protocol is a more recent training product of Japan, whose results clearly support the case to rethink stamina exercise, and the imperative of an open mind.

Performance

1 The Tabata Protocol is a systematic approach to high-intensity interval training. The idea is that several all-out intervals with minimal rest periods can produce better results than longer, lower intensity exercise. By pushing the muscles to the limit, they are forced to adapt to higher workloads. Not only does this mean that total work capacity is significantly increased, but sustained, lower-intensity efforts also become easier.

2 Stamina exercise relies on using oxygen from the air we breathe to fuel muscular work. There are three critical links in stamina exercise: the depth of breathing to fill the lungs with oxygen, the action of the heart to pump oxygen-rich blood, and the biochemical machinery of the muscles to use oxygen once it arrives. This is called the oxygen transport chain.

3 The Tabata Protocol recognises these three links and recommends whole body exercise to work as many muscles together at one

time. This produces the greatest possible workload. The heart and lungs in turn are forced to adapt, increasing their capacity to transport oxygen. This is the same response we would expect to the traditional 20-30 minute stamina sessions, three or four times each week.

4 Where Tabata stands out is that it delivers the same, or better, results in just a few minutes. After a 10-15 minute warm-up where the workload is gradually increased, you perform seven to ten high-intensity intervals. You aim to go all out for 20 to 30 seconds, then rest for 10 seconds before going at it again. The work intervals – totalling only a few minutes – are followed by a 5-minute cool down. The whole training session can be completed in around 15-20 minutes. What's more, the higher intensity of effort reduces the need for training frequency. So you only need to train like this once or twice a week.

5 Tabata works because it trades duration for intensity. Central to the success of the protocol are all-out effort and short rest intervals. Going all out, your muscles do not use oxygen to fuel activity. They have on board fuel reserves for about 20 seconds, after which they are exhausted. These reserves are recovered during the following rest period. The 10-second reprieves recommended by Tabata don't quite allow full recovery. By interval number seven or ten, you'll be at the absolute limit. This is the signal for the whole oxygen transport chain to improve. When compared with more conventional stamina training, these high intensity intervals also produce superior increases in lean muscle and reduction in body fat.

6 Many of the techniques described in the previous pages are suited to Tabata and experience will guide you in which work best for you.

Variations

You can apply this protocol to almost any stamina type exercise. Use it as an alternative to Form and Mind Boxing when you're pushed for time or need a change of pace. Once you've accumulated some experience you can ramp up the intensity further. Using chain punches and kicks, add some hand weights to increase the workload driven by the upper body. If you like running you can apply the protocol here. To begin with, simply try sprint/walk intervals. As your condition improves, the addition of small hand weights and hill work will massively increase results.

Benefits

Tabata is the hard, or external equivalent to stamina training with Form and Mind Boxing. Research demonstrates that if you want to improve your staying power, this is the most effective way to do so. There's also some metabolic magic that carries on after exercise has finished. Subjects in the Tabata trials were significantly leaner than counterparts who used steady-paced exercise. So why not use Tabata exclusively? Experience will teach you the Tabata Protocol is tough, psychologically as well as physiologically. Alternating with some Form and Mind on a regular basis prevents you becoming overstretched. Tabata will doubtless shift your conditioning up a couple of notches. Tabata also delivers an unambiguous lesson: the best results come from outright hard work forged in the fire of our will.

Chapter 5

Power Training

Basic and advanced Wu Shu exercises for developing muscle strength

"What counts is not the enormity of the task, but the size of our courage"
Matthieu Ricard

Power Training 5.0
Power – Basic and Advanced Wu Shu exercises for developing muscle strength

How power training works

Every action of our lives is dependent on muscle. Whether you're performing a complex Kung Fu move or simply sitting at rest, hundreds of muscles are working together to maintain or change the position of your limbs. Muscles are composed of thousands of individual fibres. Each fibre is packed with specialised proteins which, when activated by our nerves, cause the fibre to shorten. The shortening muscle-fibre pulls on the skeleton and this force causes the joints to move. Muscles become stronger when they are forced to work harder, or produce more force, than normal. Repeated, forceful muscle contractions signal more protein to be incorporated into the muscle, which becomes larger as a result. Larger muscles not only produce more force, but can also do more work in a given time, and are said to be more powerful.

Muscle without weight

Most of us equate building muscle with lifting weights. In this type of training the muscles are forced to work harder by lifting progressively heavier weights. While there is no doubt these exercises are effective, they require expensive equipment or access to a gym, which may be both unaffordable and inconvenient. An alternative form of power training is to work muscles against themselves, pushing the palm of one hand against the other for instance. Using our own muscles to resist our movement is called dynamic tension. We can also position ourselves so muscles have to work harder than usual. Standing in a semi-squat for instance, forces the thigh muscle to work harder due to the poor leverage of the muscle around the knee joint in this position. All of these techniques have been developed and refined by Wu Shu (Chinese martial arts) exponents over thousands of years to develop powerful muscles. They are cheap, convenient and highly effective.

Advanced power training

When a muscle has adapted to accommodate the demands imposed on it through training, it has no need to become any stronger. Only increasing the intensity of effort will stimulate further adaptation and stimulate muscle to become more powerful. Hence lifting a heavy weight will increase muscle strength, but progress will eventually stop. A significant increase in weight is required to move matters forward again. Without using weights there are several ways to increase the intensity of effort and results from your training. These techniques rely on understanding muscle function and how to apply this knowledge in practice.

Muscle can produce force in three ways: where the muscle shortens and lifts a load; where the muscle stays the same length and holds a load; and when the muscle lengthens while resisting a load. A little practical experience will soon teach you that you can hold a heavier load statically than you can lift. Equally, you can lower a much heavier weight than you can lift or hold still. Further, even when we are exhausted lifting a load, we are still able to hold it still or lower it. This points to the first means of intensifying our power training, fully exhausting our capacity to generate all types of muscle activity. Taking the press-up as an example, when you can't lift anymore, you can keep working and further stimulate your muscles by holding yourself static for as long as possible before lowering yourself.

We can also exploit the anatomical arrangement of our muscles to increase exercise intensity. In some movements the effort can be focused on a particular muscle group. Once we have driven these muscles to exhaustion, a slight shift in position can keep the pressure on while calling some additional, supporting muscles into action. This 'pre-exhaustion' technique drives further inroads into the target muscle group, stimulating greater adaptation.

All of the power-training techniques described here rely on your ability to work your muscles as hard as possible. Only when a muscle is forced to work at the limits of its tolerance will it adapt and grow stronger. A vital component of power training is therefore learning to control your muscles and their power output. Developing this skill, through a technique called 'Hard Kung', will greatly magnify your ability to generate and sustain intense effort – along with your results.

> **Benefits of power training**
>
> Training for muscle power is associated with a range of benefits. Central among these are:
>
> ◆ Every action of our lives becomes easier as we have more power at our disposal.
>
> ◆ Equally, we are capable of higher levels of physical performance for the same reason.
>
> ◆ Resistance to fatigue from high intensity effort is increased.
>
> ◆ Power training prevents the decline in bone strength and muscle strength with age.
>
> ◆ Power training increases muscle mass and metabolic rate, enhancing the effectiveness of any weight-loss regimes.

Using these exercises

These exercises are designed to systematically develop power in all of the major muscles groups. Each level of exercise lays the building blocks for the next, so use them in order. Learning the skills of dynamic tension equips you with a powerful muscle-building tool you can take anywhere. Neglecting this skill only deprives you of your potential. Equally, results take time, but if you work conscientiously and patiently, progress will come.

Guidelines for power training

Interestingly, the widely accepted 'rules' for strength training have little scientific basis. Forceful muscle contractions are essential, but an absolute formula does not exist. Experience will guide you, but based on traditional methods some good pointers are:

- Warm up and finish with some light exercise to prevent strains and enhance recovery.

- Exercise somewhere you can concentrate fully on what you are doing.

- Focus your attention on the muscles you want to exercise.

- Breathe steadily throughout your power-training exercises and do not hold your breath.

- Exercise large muscle groups, like the legs, first because this requires more effort.

- Move slowly in each exercise, concentrating on maintaining the tension in your muscles.

- Exercise at an intensity that results in causing your muscle to shake slightly – this means you are getting the most powerful muscle fibres to work hard.

- Push yourself. Muscles only get stronger if they are forced to work to their limit.

- Intense muscular exercise is tough and you should expect it to feel uncomfortable. This said, stop exercise at once if you experience pain.

Masters Mind and Body: Advanced Kung Fu techniques for personal transformation

Level White

Power Training 5.1
Basic power exercises

Explanation

Prior to teaching a new student any fighting technique, Masters would often insist on a prolonged period of intensive physical training and preparation. The Horse Stance, press-up and abdominal curl are fundamental training stance for a huge number of martial arts. The Horse Stance develops power and flexibility in the lower limbs as a strong foundation other stances. The Golden Bridge is a hand form often used in conjunction with the Horse Stance to help to condition the upper limbs. Much of the power for striking out with the hand or arm comes from the waist, the muscles of which also support the back and upper body stability. The abdominal curl is a simple, but extremely effective exercise for the midsection. Because striking power is transmitted to an opponent through the arms, upper-body strength is a key component of Kung Fu training. Taming the Tiger is similar to the regular press-up, but has some subtle differences from press-ups that make it a more productive exercise.

Performance

1 Open the Character Two stance. Then perform the same sequence of feet movements again, so you end with your feet

twice shoulder width apart. Keeping your back straight, sink your bottom down until your thighs are almost parallel with the floor. There is a tendency to lean forward and let the bottom stick out, so concentrate on pushing your pelvis forward and keep the back straight. Place both hands in front of your chest, palms facing forward and fingers upward. Curl the fingers inward so only your index finger points straight up. Point your thumbs toward each other so the thumbs and index finger form an 'L-shape'. Hold this final position breathing slowing and steadily. Focus on maintaining your hand position and keeping your legs still. Hold this position for 30 seconds and work up to a minute by adding 10 seconds every day or so you practise. Work up to holding the Golden Bridge for three minutes or so.

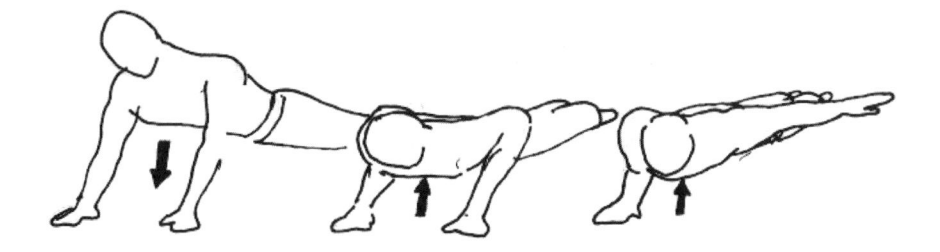

2 Lie face down with your palms on the floor beside your chest and elbows pointing back towards your feet. Makes sure you are resting on the instep of the foot. Slowly push your body off the floor taking a count of five to extend the arms fully. Begin to lower your body at the same rate, but stop halfway down and hold this position for a count of five before continuing to lower yourself to the floor. Start out with 5-7 repetitions, gradually working up to 15-20.

3 Lie on the floor, placing your hands on your chest and drawing your feet up toward your buttocks. Slowly lift your head, moving your chin to your chest. Then lift your upper back off the floor. You should only be able to move an inch or two. Hold the final position for a second and then slowly lower yourself back to the starting position. Lifting and lowering should take about two seconds each. Start out with 5-7 repetitions, adding one a day until you can do 30 or more.

Variations

The Golden Bridge, given its static nature, doesn't really have many variations. You may however, find it easier to omit the arm action to start. On the other hand 'Tame the Tiger' has plenty of scope for growth. If you find it too hard to begin with, try performing the exercise leaning up against a wall, gradually moving your feet further back, so your body forms a greater angle with the wall. If you are very strong, or want more challenge, add more stops as you lift and lower yourself. One-handed 'Taming' is performed with the hand of the 'resting' arm held behind the head, touching the elbow on the floor at the end of the lowering phase. The final evolution is holding the 'resting' arm straight out to your side and touch the floor with your palm at the bottom of the repetition. The abdominal curl also lends itself to development. You can add intensity to the curl by placing your hands on your shoulders and then stretching them out behind you. You can also move and hold the contracted position for extended periods and also try not fully relaxing as you unfold to the starting position. Equally, you can emphasise one side of your tummy by adding a slight twist at the top of the movement, pulling the right shoulder toward the left hip and so on.

Benefits

The tension created in the thighs and forearms from The Golden Bridge speaks for itself. Early and continued practice of this simple and effective exercise, as with the others described here, will serve you well. You'll soon notice how the added power translates to easier kicking, climbing stairs and walking. Taming the Tiger will build tremendous power into your upper body. This will translate to other exercises, such as more powerful chain punches when stamina training, and the ease with which any daily activities involving carrying can be accomplished. The midsection is the pivot around which the body turns. You'll soon find that regular practice of the abdominal curl will improve your performance in almost any activity. Your chances of back injury will fade dramatically, as will your waistline.

Power Training 5.2
The Warrior Stance

Explanation

Stance training serves a variety of purposes for the martial artist. Their principle purpose is to illustrate how power is developed in the legs for particular fighting movements. When striking forward, the power is generated by straightening the back leg to push the foot into the ground. The front leg bends to allow the force to move forward, with the momentum translated through the midsection to the lead arm. Stance training exaggerates the movements used in real fighting not just to underscore their mechanics but also to build power into the muscles involved in the movement. The Warrior Stance trains the leg muscle used in a forward stance combined with an arm position designed to build power into the muscles of the back and shoulders.

Performance

1 Stand in a relaxed posture, feet shoulder width apart, hands by your sides. Take a few slow, deep abdominal breaths.

2 Keeping your hips square, take a giant step forward. Keep lowering your hips until your front thigh is parallel to the ground. When you look down, your front knee should be over your front foot. Straighten your rear leg, allowing the rear foot to turn outward so the entire sole is in contact with the ground.

3 Bring your hands in front of your chest, palms facing each other, finger together and pointing upward. Press your hands overhead until your elbows are straight and alongside your ears.

4 Keeping your elbows close to your ears and your arms straight try to pull your hands backwards as far as they will go. You'll feel tremendous tension in our shoulders when you're doing it right.

5 Start on your left leg and hold for 30 seconds before shifting to the right leg. Work up to five minutes or more held on each leg.

Variations

You can omit the arm movement at first if you find the whole thing difficult to coordinate. Don't leave it altogether as it is an important element of the exercise. You can increase the difficulty (and value) of the arm work by turning your hands palm up in the final position, with the fingers pointing backward. While you pull your arms back with your shoulders, try to push the heel of your palm upward while pulling your fingertips down toward your shoulder (like lifting a heavy object overhead). For a change from static stance holding, you can use the giant step in a more dynamic way by pushing immediately back to standing upright and repeating on the opposite leg for as many repetitions as you can handle.

Benefits

Effective fighting derives power through the stance and translates its effect through the arms. This relies on powerful legs, midsection and shoulders; all developed with ample reserve in The Warrior. Almost every muscle group in your body will be reached by this exercise. Equally generalised returns will soon appear in the form of improved flexibility, poise and power.

Power Training 5.3
The Iron Bridge

Explanation

Much of the power expressed through hand techniques is developed through the legs, and particularly the hips. Equally, a solid stance is absolutely essential to prevent us being pushed back by our own force when we strike. The vital link between the legs and arms is the midsection, referred to as 'The Bridge' in Chinese Kung Fu. The Bridge facilitates the flow of power generated by the legs to drive the arms, and in addition protects the internal organs if you have to take a punch. A weak 'Bridge' inevitably leads you, and your techniques, vulnerable to folding under pressure. The Iron Bridge is a deceptively simple, but highly effective remedy to a soggy midsection.

Performance

1 Lay on your back with your arms at your side. Take a few slow, deep abdominal breaths.

2 Now two things happen at once. Keeping your legs straight and knees locked, lift your feet and inch or two from the ground. At the same time lift your head and shoulder slightly off the ground. You should feel tension along the entire front of your body.

3 Be sure to keep breathing slowly and deeply, avoid the temptation to hold your breath.

4 Hold this position for 30 seconds, then slowly relax. Take a break for a minute or so before repeating for another 30 seconds.

5 Work up to holding The Iron Bridge for three minutes or more.

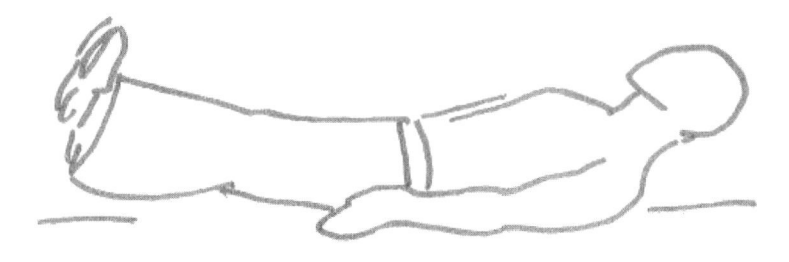

Variations

The Iron Bridge can be trained to benefit the muscles of the back. Simply reverse the process by lifting your bottom off the ground, supporting your weight on your shoulders and feet. When you can hold the Bridge for three minutes you can make the exercise tougher by holding yourself between two chairs. Place your head and shoulders on one chair, then lift your feet up onto one opposite and straighten the whole body using the power of your midsection.

Benefits

Powerful waist muscles support the lower spine, preventing injury when lifting a heavy object or twisting suddenly. Thousands succumb to such injury every year, often resulting in prolonged periods of pain and debilitation. You could, of course, elect to avoid these activities altogether, choosing a passive back-care strategy. Inactivity is inevitably accompanied by deterioration in midsection power over time, inexorably drawing you toward a date with disaster. Aggressive care of the back, through early and continued practice of The Iron Bridge, will prevent torn muscles, popped discs and keep you fiercely active well into old age.

Power Training 5.4
The Golden Dragon

Explanation

The training stances develop power in the lower limbs by forcing the leg muscles to hold the joints in position of extreme mechanical disadvantage. The same principle can be applied with the upper body by holding the mid-point of a press-up. The Golden Dragon is the final evolution of this idea, demanding enormous effort from the arms and entire shoulder girdle to hold the body in the cruciform position. The midsection and legs are also called forcefully into play holding the body rigid. In fact, after your first attempt you'll have a job to find any muscles that don't suffer next-day tenderness. Cruciform does derive from a word meaning punish and torture after all.

Performance

1 Kneel on the floor and take a few deep breaths. Calm your mind and focus.

2 Assume a press-up position with your hands spaced wider than your shoulders.

3 Rather than supporting yourself on the ball of your foot, as in regular press-ups, use the instep – this makes things harder.

4 Keep your body straight throughout, revisiting the urge to bend or sag in the middle.

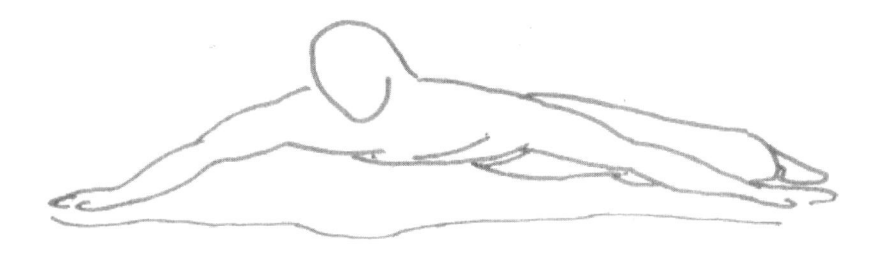

5 Hold this position for 30 seconds and then lower yourself to the floor. Rest for 30 seconds and start again. Work up to holding this position for a whole minute.

6 As your strength improves, adopt a wider hand spacing until you can hold your chest just a few inches off the floor for the full minute.

Variations

If you find this one too tough to start, try supporting your weight on your knees rather than your instep. You can use a variant of this exercise to work the muscles of your back. Start by laying on your front, feet together and hands outstretched to you sides. Then lift your head, hand and feet a few inches from the floor and hold. The Golden Dragon also works lying on your back, although only the strongest can actually lift themselves off the ground. To perform the reverse version, simply lie on your back in the cruciform position. Press down with the back of your hands and feet, lifting your bottom off the floor.

Benefits

It's hard to pin down a 'best' overall exercise, but this one might just get my nod. The Golden Bridge, the equivalent exercise for the lower body, would also challenge for first place. These exercises are simple, convenient and extraordinarily effective. Between the two, you're going to demand almost every muscle in your body gives everything it's got.

Power Training 5.5
Praying to Buddha Stance

Explanation

One-legged stance training appears in many forms of Kung Fu – with the White Crane making a cameo in more than a few martial arts movies. Great Masters would often insist new students practised little else at the outset of their training, as much to test determination and character as to develop physical condition. Praying to Buddha is among the most evolved of the training stances, and takes its name from the images of the cross-legged Buddha. Not only is this stance physically tough, your determination also gets a thorough workout fighting the urge to quit. Beyond their distinctly inscrutable flavour, one-legged training stances build poise, balance and strength, which translates to greater power and stability when moving and kicking. In common with other training stances, the legs are positioned to place the muscles of the hip and thigh at a severe mechanical disadvantage. Shifting the entire body weight from two legs onto one forces the muscles to work at the limits of their power.

Performance

1 Stand in a relaxed posture, feet shoulder width apart, hands by your sides. Take a few slow, deep abdominal breaths.

2 Shift your weight on to the left foot. Bend your knee and sink down a few inches.

3 Lift the right foot off the ground. When you've caught your balance, place the right foot on top of your left knee, just as if you were crossing your legs.

4 Place your palms together with the fingers pointing up. Your fingertips should be level with your nose. Your elbows should point out to the side with your forearms parallel to the floor.

5 Sink down as low as you can and hold yourself still. Take long, slow abdominal breaths.

6 Begin with 30 seconds on each leg and gradually work up until you can stand for 3 minutes or more. Then concentrate on sinking lower as your condition improves.

Variations

To make this a more complete, whole-body exercise, you can try forcefully pressing your palms together while holding the stance. Be sure to keep breathing deeply and steadily, resisting the tendency to hold your breath. Of course, you can adopt any arm position you want while remaining true to the basic form, or leave it out altogether. For the adepts who want a really fierce challenge, you can stop giving the crossed leg a free ride and stretch it out straight in front of you.

Benefits

Although Praying to Buddha is probably the most effective exercise for building power into the lower limbs without using weights, its greatest benefit is probably psychological. There is simply no getting away from how difficult this stance is. No change of scenery, no distraction and no movement to relieve the discomfort in your muscles – just you and the stance. Your thighs may firm up from Praying to Buddha, but your determination will become forged in iron.

Power Training 5.6
Sleeping Louhan Rolls Over

Level Red

Explanation

Many martial arts moves demand rapid changes of direction and twisting action about the waist. This places a tremendous strain on the lower back and, without proper control, potential for injury. Twisting the waist is driven by the muscles on the side of your tummy; called the obliques. The fibres of these muscles are arranged at an angle (an oblique one) so that when they contract, the ribs on one side of the body are pulled toward the pelvis on the opposite side. Developing the oblique muscles lends increased power and control to twisting movements. This not only means you can accomplish more rapid changes of direction, and potential exercise workloads, but do so while studiously avoiding injury to the lower spine.

Performance

1 Lie on the floor and tuck your feet under a table or some other heavy furniture. Your knees should be bent and feet drawn up close to your bottom.

2 Push your hands straight out in front of you. Clear your mind and take a couple of slow, deep abdominal breaths.

3 Breathe out steadily and sit up until only your lower back is in contact with the floor. You will feel the muscles on the front of your tummy tense up. Keep breathing steadily through the tension.

4 Keeping your arms out and back straight, twist slowly around to your left until your fingers touch the floor. Hold this position for a second or two before returning, equally slowly to the starting position.

5 Keeping your breathing slow and steady, repeat on the right side.

6 Alternate twists from side to side. Start with three repetitions on each side and gradually work up to five, ten then 20.

Variations

You can make this exercise tougher by concentrating all the effort, and repetitions, on one side at a time. Equally, once you have reached 20 or so comfortable repetitions, carrying a heavy book in your outstretched hands takes the intensity of effort to new levels. You can also exercise the oblique muscles by reversing the end of your body that twists. Try lying flat on the floor, lifting your legs straight up (so you form an 'L' shape) and then lowering your feet to the left and right.

Benefits

Sleeping Louhan Rolls Over will develop enormous strength into the muscles on the side of your waist. This will translate to greater control and power in your stamina training. The supporting effect of these muscles on the lower spine will improve posture and poise during your power exercises. Combined with the static contract demanded from your frontal tummy muscles, this is among the most productive of all abdominal exercises.

Power Training 5.7
The Falling Leaf

Explanation

The martial artist who wins every fight without getting a beating only appears in movies. Realistically, an essential part of fighting is learning how to get knocked over without getting knocked out. There are a whole range of techniques to absorb the impact as you meet the floor following a trip or throw, The Falling Leaf exercise trains the muscles of the upper body to break the fall if you get pushed over forward. This exercise also demonstrates an extremely important fact about muscle function. Essentially, there are three types of muscular work: where the muscle shortens; holds something statically in place; and where the muscle is forced to lengthen because the load is too heavy. Intuitively you may already have realised you can hold more weight in place than you can lift. When you max-out on press-ups for instance, you reach a point where you can't lift your body weight any more, but can hold it in a static position for a bit longer. It is equally true that you can lower something heavier than you can lift. During Falling Leaf your upper body will be forced to work harder than a regular press-up, lowering your body weight multiplied by its momentum toward the ground. This exercise therefore multiplies the potential training effects of the press-up.

Performance

1 Stand in a relaxed posture, feet shoulder width apart, hands by your sides. Take a few slow, deep abdominal breaths.

2 Put your arms out in front of you, palms facing forward.

3 Keeping your body as straight as possible, simply fall forward into a press-up position.

4 Using your arms like shock absorbers, break the descent and lower yourself toward the floor.

5 Just before reaching the floor, straighten your arms as hard as you can and press yourself back up.

6 Stand up and repeat the whole process. Start with one repetition at a time, composing yourself before each Falling Leaf. Gradually work up to a sequence of five, then ten and finally 20 repetitions without a break.

Variations

If you find the idea of throwing yourself at the ground a little overwhelming, start out falling forward from the kneeling position. Work up to the standing start when you're ready. When you master the Falling Leaf you can augment its benefits by putting more into the push-up motion. Try to explode out of the lowest position, as if jumping off your hands, until you can push yourself clean off the floor. Of course, you can apply the same principle to your leg exercise. You can get a similar effect jumping down from a step. The higher the step, the greater your momentum, and effort required, to break the fall. Throwing in a vertical jump straight after landing finishes the 'depth jump'.

Benefits

This exercise not only tests the limits of upper-body power, but also adds a new dimension in the form of negative, or lowering, muscular activity. Knowledge is power, and understanding different forms of muscle activity more fully will help you get more from your exercise.

Power Training 5.8
Advanced Power Training

Explanation

Muscle is stubborn. Your body doesn't want to have any more than the minimum necessary. This is because muscle in very inefficient. It is an active tissue whose maintenance, let alone work, demands more energy per day than any other organ in your body. When you can achieve a particular workload, your muscles stop adapting. This allows you to accommodate a specific effort in the most economical way. Your body will only acquire muscle if it absolutely has to. In order to signal a muscle to grow stronger, you have to repeatedly push it further than it's gone before. There are a variety of techniques that can help us intensify muscular effort. This helps us push beyond our normal limitations. One consequence of muscle's innate inefficiency is that as effort shifts up a gear, speed of recovery does not keep pace. Balancing increasing intensity and recovery is the key to further progress.

Performance

1 The simplest way to drive your muscles harder is to try and perform more repetitions of a particular exercise. This could mean more Taming the Tiger, abdominal curls or longer holding The Golden Bridge.

2 You can drive intensity up a notch with additional resistance. This does not mean you need to have access to expensive weight training equipment. A backpack filled with books, canned food or water bottles ads a new dimension to stance training and Taming the Tiger. Clutched across your chest or held at arm's length, the same improvised 'weight' greatly intensifies abdominal curls and The Golden Bridge.

3 Your muscles are actually weakest in the normal lifting phase of a movement. This is the pressing-up phase of Taming the Tiger. You can actually hold more weight statically than you can lift. So, when you can't grind out one more repetition, simply hold till you drop.

4 The strongest phase of any lift is the lowering portion, when the muscle is lengthening. Just because you can't manage another press-up, or even hold yourself static, you can lower yourself under control a few times or perform Falling Leaf. The same applies to stance training and the leg exercises illustrated previously. So, when you can't hold The Golden Bridge any longer, lunge into The Warrior Stance on each leg a few times or use the depth jump.

5 When you've gone as far as you can go with a particular exercise, you can push still further by calling in the assistance of additional muscles. The Golden Dragon focuses tremendous effort on the chest muscles. When these muscles are fatigued you can move into the standard press-up position and hold a little longer. This is because the latter posture calls into action additional, fresh muscles from the arms and back. Applying the same logic to the legs, having pushed Praying to Buddha as far as it will go, dropping into The Golden Bridge enlists fresh muscles from the resting leg.

6 It is important to realise that recovery ability is strictly limited. There is only so much resource to meet the demands of daily life, including exercise. The harder you push, in all areas of your life, the longer you will need to recover. Your muscles may require several days between intense training to fully recover and adapt. Fatigue and progress are your best guides here. Too much of the former and lack of the latter suggest bigger gaps between training sessions.

Variations

You can apply these techniques to almost every power training exercise in this book. You can elect to apply one technique, such as negative work or static holds, or use them all at once.

Benefits

This range of intensifying techniques represents a power-training toolbox. You can use these tools to beef up a particular exercise, focus on a particular facet of strength and power, or simply add variety and interest to your program.

Power Training 5.9
Hard Kung training

Explanation

Strangely, the person with the largest muscles is not always strongest. We've all had the experience of meeting someone slightly built who can exert tremendous power. An essential component of power is the control we can demonstrate over our muscles. The link between our will and our muscles varies considerably from person to person, and is largely fixed before birth. Within our individual, predetermined limits, power training develops the inherent force that our muscles can generate and the level of control our will can exert over them. This training is however, highly specific. Simply because we have developed strength in one movement, it does not automatically translate into a similar improvement in other activities.

Many of the strength-training exercises described previously take advantage of poor leverage to work muscles harder than normal. As you have progressed, you have become more powerful at those exercises. Hard Kung is a technique developed to bridge the gap between the power you have acquired and its expression in other activities. Once again, the concept of Chi is central to this form of training. The idea is that unification of breath, will and action optimises Chi flow to the limbs and increases their striking power. For those who would rather not consider the role, or even existence of Chi, this approach to improved neurological efficiency is still well supported within the objective confines of modern science.

If you've ever wondered why martial artists shout when they strike, the idea is to unify breath, action and Chi. Particular noises are associated with directing Chi to the attacking limb and into your opponent; 'Huh!' for the hands and 'Ahh!' to the lower extremities. It also scares the pants off most attackers!

Physiologically, shouting causes forceful contraction of the diaphragm and makes us breathe out. This prevents breath holding, which usually accompanies all-out effort and can cause a precipitous rise in blood pressure. It also tenses the muscles of the abdomen, supporting the spine when high forces are exerted between the upper and lower body. There is some evidence that reflex pathways sense the additional protection for the lower back, facilitating full expression of otherwise injurious levels of muscular power. Psychologically, shouting is a very liberating and healthy conduit to express any negative feelings you might be carrying around with you.

Performance

1 Open the Character Two Stance and assume the on guard position. Take a few deep, abdominal breaths. As you breath in, imagine you are accumulating energy in your lower abdomen. As you breath out, imagine that energy flowing up your spine, through your shoulders and down your arms to your hands.

2 Drive a single punch forward from your rear hand as hard as you can. Be sure to keep your shoulders square. Breath out forcefully, making a 'Huh!' sounds. Take a deep abdominal breath, repeating the visualisation, and drive a punch forward from the opposite hand. Work up through five, ten to 30 repetitions.

3 Draw you fists to your sides, palms up, keeping your elbows back and close to your body. Breath out and drive both fists forward as hard as you can. Take a breath, then pull your fists to your side, forcefully driving your elbows backward. Work up through five, ten to 30 repetitions.

4 Breath in and slowly push your hands in front of your chest so the wrists cross about six inches in front of your nose. Keep lifting your arms up until your crossed hands are above your head. Imagine power rushing down your arms to your fists. Now swing your arms out and down in a big circle, smashing your fists down to your side. As you do so, breathe out forcefully and drop your weight into the strike.

5 Drop into a Horse Stance, pulling your fists to your sides. Take a deep breath, visualizing power driving down into your legs. Push your weight back onto your right leg and kick out to the side as hard as you can with your left leg. As you kick, breathe out forcefully, making an 'Aah!' noise and punch out with the arm on the same side. Recover the kick and drop back into the starting position. Work up to 30 repetitions on each side.

6 From the Horse Stance breathe in and push your weight back onto your right leg. Standing on your right leg, lift your left knee as high as you can. Now, breath out and drive forward into a Warrior Stance leading with your left leg. As your foot touches down drive both your fists forward into and punch as hard as you can. Imagine power driving through your arms and out of your fists. If it helps, think about smashing through a brick wall! The whole movement should coincide with breathing out forcefully, making an 'Aah!' sound.

Variations

You can make your Hard Kung more intense in several ways. Performing more repetitions in the same time, without compromising on power, demands a massive increase in workload and intensity. The addition of hand weight takes your effort up a couple of notches, especially if you keep up the speed of movement. The visualization is a key element of Hard Kung. Even if you don't accept the idea of Chi, the mental imagery certainly boosts coordination and the expression of muscular power. If you feel self-conscious about shouting, or can't shout without scaring your neighbours, dispense with the noise and simply breathe out forcefully as you strike.

Benefits

Hard Kung trains the link between the intrinsic power of your muscles and your will to express their full potential. Once mastered, you can apply the Hard Kung principle to improve your power in almost any movement or activity.

Chapter 6

Special Situations

Integration – personalising your program

> "Everything flows and nothing stays,
> we cannot step twice into the same river"
> — Heraclitus

Special Situations 6.0
Integration – personalising your program

Explanation

If you're a reader of the fitness press, you'd get the impression that the latest training plans were built on some precise insight. So many repetitions, for so long, so many times each week produces such-and-such a result. The simple truth is that exercise science has not delivered such a refined equation for self-improvement. When you get right down to it, nobody is entirely sure of the exact mechanisms by which exercise promotes its effects (a fact frequently exploited by faddists!). While the evidence we have can put us in the ballpark, we can't be absolutely certain of the best training strategies. When you mix in some individual differences and genetic predispositions, a specific prescription becomes virtually impossible. Fortunately, there are some useful guidelines to direct your training. These are logical benchmarks against which you can measure the success of your efforts and implement changes to your program to make it even more effective.

Performance

1 Identity. You have innumerable characteristics which single you out from the crowd and unmistakably define you, as you. Similarly, each of your physiological and psychological functions has a specific identity. This identity not only defines the purpose of each function, but suggests how it must be trained to improve. For example, muscles produce force, which tells us we have to lift heavy weights to train them. Body fat deposits excess energy consumed in food, telling us we have to create a deficit to reduce stores of fat in our body.

2 Potential. We are all different. Each of us has predefined genetic limits on our trainability, whether it's physical or mental. This not only defines the range to which we can extend ourselves, but the effort that is required to do so.

3 Specific adaptation to imposed demands. Training must be as specific as possible. If you want to become stronger, lift heavy weights. If you want to become stronger in a particular movement, work with heavy weights in that specific movement. Equally, don't expect to become stronger running marathon races, where the imposed demands are different. These would be better suited to creating an energy deficit to reduce body fat.

4 Adequate stimulus. Once you've set in motion the process of adaptation with specific demands, you don't need to keep on doing it. Essentially, you only need so much exercise to bring on change. Once you've accomplished this for yourself, more is not better. Of course, what is an adequate stimulus depends on the specific training effect you want. The stimulus for building bigger muscles is lifting heavy weights till exhaustion. Similarly, the stimulus for greater stamina is to persist in an activity for longer than you have before.

5 Progressive overload. You will not improve if you train at a level you can already accommodate. For example, your muscles have no need to become bigger and stronger if you lift weights you can already handle. The intensity of effort, whatever you're training, must overload your current capacity. Improvements accommodate the new training demands, so you must progressively increase intensity to keep moving forward.

6 Restoration. Exercise is a negative. Its demands drain your physical and mental reserves. This fatigue is the stimulus for your body to adapt. Improvement only comes if you allow yourself time to recover. This can be several days after intense exercise, but only a few hours following everyday activities. Once again, more is not better. If you train again before you've recovered, this simply makes further inroads into your reserves and prevents improvement. It's also important to realise that recovery ability is limited. It does not distinguish between the demands placed on it by your life. For example, if you're having a hard time at work, you may not recover from exercise as fast as when you're on holiday.

7 Readiness. The ideal point to train again is when recovered and willing to overload yourself. Typically, the more frequently and intensely you train in an activity, the longer the period of restoration before you're ready to go again. Readiness is not simply limited by physical fatigue, but also includes a range of psychological imponderables. Even though we are fatigued from one form of training, power training for instance, we may be ready for another whose demands are different, such as stamina training. As adaptation requires intense effort to produce overload, this suggests you'll get the best results from training hard with a variety of activities. This strategy will give you the best opportunity to be recovered and ready to give each exercise bout your best.

8 Reversibility. The corollary of readiness is reversibility. If you leave it too long before you exercise again, you peak and then start to lose your improvements. Eventually, you end up right back where you started. Assuming you train hard, the trick is to train often enough, balanced against the demands of your life at the time, to keep improving.

9 Periodisation. The results of even the best-designed training programs inevitably grind to a halt. This can be due to cumulative fatigue, poor recovery due to life demands, or just plain boredom. Not surprisingly, readiness frequently drops off when we're repeatedly faced with the prospect of thankless, intense effort. When results are slow coming, frustration leads many to quit altogether. The trick is to work hard for a short period of time, then back off a bit to enjoy the rewards of your efforts. Regular cycles of hard and easy training help us stay ready, committed and enthusiastic. Cycles can take the form of alternating hard-easy days, weeks or months, whatever works for you.

Variations

You can broadly apply these ideas to any type of training, physical or mental. They work pretty well as a benchmark for your efforts to reach most goals, in fact.

Benefits

Reaching for a goal can often be like groping in the dark – often it is difficult to know if we're going in the right direction. These guidelines allow you to critically evaluate your strategy to reach any training goal (or one recommended to you). If your results are not all they should be, they provide a benchmark against which to assess the potential effectiveness of changes to your plan. As opposed being a blind follower of others, you have the tools to confidently take the lead in shaping your own future.

Special situations 6.1
Model Routines

Explanation

The Mind and Body Metamorphosis program not only develops a high level of conditioning, but the skills to build your own routine directed toward specific objectives. Until you find your feet, it's often useful to have a track to run on. The following is a model routine mapped out over a typical week of training. This routine uses all the major themes covered in this book to deliver a varied, interesting and well-rounded program, omitting none of the major fitness components.

Training Program

Day	Exercise	Objective	Application
1	Basic kicks and punches Basic strength training	Essential conditioning	For beginners and building basic stamina before moving into optimum conditioning
2	Off		
3	Tabata Protocol Hard Kung	Optimum conditioning	Use if you're in a hurry or building power or going after peak condition
4	Off		
5	Form and Mind Boxing Eight Pieces of Brocade	Focus and relaxation	Use for relaxation, perfecting technique and to help recovery from optimum conditioning
6	Off		
7	Off		

Of course, one size does not fit all, and you may have specific training requirements. There is no reason you cannot emphasis a particular type of training to suit your needs. If you have very little time for example, you need to get the maximum impact from every exercise minute you invest. In this case, the Tabata Protocol is the way to go. On the other hand, you may simply need something to take your mind from pressing problems and give you pause to regroup. Form and Mind, balanced with The Eight Pieces of Brocade, will do nicely.

Variations

The model routine delivers a week of varied intensity, but you can apply the same idea from week to week, or over several months. This is a technique called Periodisation. The basic idea is that you have phases where you give it your all for optimum conditioning, then back off for a while. Your period of all-out effort is preceded by a spell of basic conditioning and followed by a more relaxed recovery phase.

Benefits

Even within the confines of the model routine, you can direct your efforts to meet personal goals. Periodisation has been demonstrated to help even very well-conditioned athletes achieve greater results. The discrete phases of training help facilitate stronger focus and greater effort toward your goals. Taking these broad principles you can explore almost limitless permutations in your training, ensuring it remains consistently fresh, interesting and enjoyable.

Special situation 6.2
Deskbound. Down, but not out

Explanation

The past hundred years saw a massive improvement in our health, increase in life expectancy and the free time to enjoy it. This was largely facilitated by parallel advances in technology. Many forms of work that demanded hours of intense manual labour have been transformed by mechanisation into little more than the flick of switch. Computer software opens travel to exotic locations and experience of hazardous activities in confines of virtual reality, safe in the comfort of an armchair, never moving a muscle.

Unfortunately, our physical constitution and mental hard wiring has not kept pace with technology. We are little more evolved than they were millions of years ago, when life demanded physical activity and provided tangible outcomes from it. We are poorly adapted to sedentary existence and a virtual world. This fact is increasingly manifesting itself through an obvious trend toward obesity, poor condition and anxiety.

Most of us spend the vast majority of our time deskbound and sitting, and this is a key culprit in our progressive physical decline. Prolonged periods of sitting have both short-term and further reaching consequences for our well-being. There is a tendency to slump, round-shouldered, which inhibits natural breathing and undermines the postural integrity of the back. In the longer term the deskbound lifestyles promotes significant de-conditioning, leading to obesity and premature aging.

In many ways we have become victims of our own evolutionary success. The cost of our progress is the need to compensate with regular physical activity. Sitting at work clearly presents a significant challenge to your conditioning, but does not condemn it altogether. Coupled with a commitment to regular exercise, deskbound can simply become another opportunity for mastery.

Performance

1 Sit upright, palms on top of your legs, with the thumbs on the outside of your thighs. Your elbows should stick out to the side. Push your bottom to the back of the chair and straighten your back. Press your palms down on your thighs and push your chest up. As you do so, take a deep breath in. Relax and breathe out.

2 Keeping the same position, place your palms over your navel. As you breathe out, gently press on your tummy and pull it in. As you breathe in, let your tummy expand. Practise taking these abdominal breaths while keeping an upright posture.

3 Keeping the same posture, lift your arms straight out in front of you and make your hands into a fist. Take a deep abdominal breath. As you breathe out clench your fists as tight as you can. Practise five to ten repetitions to start, working up to 49 times as your condition improves. Repeat the sequence with your arms held straight overhead, out to the side and then hanging straight down by your waist.

4 Take a deep abdominal breath. As you breathe out, look back over your right shoulder and twist around from the waist, keeping your hips square to the front. As you do so, reach across your chest with your left hand and as far back to the right as you can. Hold this position for a few seconds then return to face front. Repeat left and right five to ten times, working up to 49 times as your condition improves.

5 Place your feet together, flat on the floor so they are just under the front rim of your seat. Take a deep abdominal breath. As you breathe out use your legs to lift your bottom an inch or so from your seat and hold in this position. Stay there for a slow count of ten, and then slowly lower yourself back into the seat. Work up to holding this position for 10, 20, 30 seconds or more.

6 Shift your bottom to the front of your seat. Spread your feet about twice shoulder-width apart, so your thighs form a 45-degree angle. Take a deep abdominal breath. As you breathe out, use your legs to lift your bottom an inch or so from your seat

and hold in this position. Stay there for a slow count of ten, and then slowly lower yourself back into the seat. Work up to holding this position for 10, 20, 30 seconds or more.

7   Place your palms on your armrests or the side of your seat. Take a deep abdominal breath. As you breathe out try and lift your knees toward your chest. Hold for a second or two and relax. Repeat five to ten times. When you can easily perform ten or more lifts, try performing this exercise holding your legs straight out in front of you.

8   Place your palms on your armrests or the side of your seat. Take a deep abdominal breath. As you breathe out press down and try to lift yourself from your seat. Repeat five to ten times.

9   Grab hold of the side of your seat. Take a deep abdominal breath. As you breathe out, try and pull yourself down into the seat. Hold for a second or two and relax. Repeat five to ten times.

10 Place your palms flat on your desk with your arms straight. Take a deep abdominal breath. As you breath out press your palms down forcefully, being sure to keep your elbows straight. Hold for a second or two and relax. Practice five to ten repetitions to start, working up to 49 times as your condition improves.

Variations

A commonsense variation, which almost doesn't bear pointing out because it's so obvious, is try to stand up whenever you can. The very act of standing significantly reduces some physiological damage wrought by sitting all day. You can further increase the value of standing by adopting the Character Two Stance. As described in the Stamina Training section of this volume, this stance offers a thorough – and discreet – workout for your thighs and hips while you're standing and chatting on the telephone. You can also try the sitting version of The Eight Pieces of Brocade described in the Chi Kung section of this book. This was specifically designed to aid recovery for bedridden wounded soldiers, but works equally well for the morbidly deskbound.

Finally, when your condition improves, you can add resistance. Holding a loaded briefcase or few reams of paper at arm's length while standing away from your chair reaches a few muscles that are rarely used in the office environment.

Benefits

These exercises cannot replace a structured program of regular exercise. They can help prevent, or at least slow, the worst effects of a sedentary lifestyle. If nothing else, a few moves every hour or so helps focus the mind on the need for more exercise when time permits. Spread throughout the day, an occasional bout of squeezes, stretches and lifts also offer a pleasant break from work to help us stay fresh and focused.

Notes

Corporate Testimonials

29 January 2008
Thanks so much for coming out to share your experience with us.
Your presentation was very well received, leaving the group both energized and excited by the content. There was also much comment on the relevance of the messages you portrayed to our own conference – it brought the whole concept of lean six sigma to life in a way that really helped everyone engage with it.

Oliver Coleshill
HR & Training Manager, Benugo

17 December 2007
Matt provided a one-hour session on mind and body 'metamorphosis' for the Peverel Group Personnel and Payroll team of around 45 people at their two-day conference. In spite of it being at the end of a long and tiring day Matt used his magic to work high levels of energy into the room from a relatively gentle start. Everybody who took part was very actively engaged with the exercises and at times it became quite competitive as he got people working in two teams. Matt got them to make the appropriate noises while using the martial arts techniques he was teaching and the noise became quite deafening in the room as everybody threw themselves into it. Following the event, feedback was extremely positive with everybody having enjoyed the session and, using his book which was provided to everybody, some have gone on to continue practising in the comfort of their own homes.
Thank you Matt for a really successful session!

Emma Phelps
Group Training and Development Manager, Peverel Group

November 2006
Thank you Matt, for an insightful, fun and challenging team-building event. It was great to do something different with our marketing team and to link it with a discipline that has resonance with our parent company Honda. Plus we all enjoyed doing something slightly out
of the ordinary.

Alastair Watkins
Marketing Manager, Honda Racing F1 Team

Masters Mind & Body does not deal with fighting. If you are interested in finding out more about the combat side of the techniques described here, I highly recommend Alan Gibson's *Beginning Wing Chun* (ISBN 978-1-84024-546-2) as one of the best introductions to Chinese Kung Fu available.

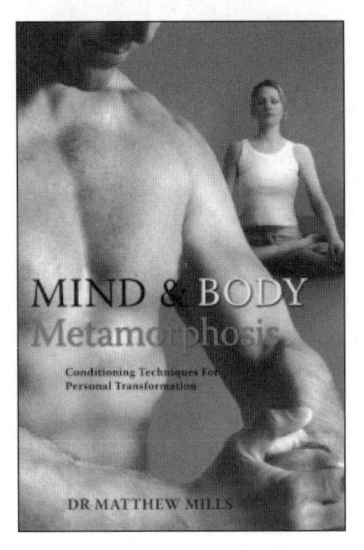

Masters Mind & Body builds on the basic techniques shown in the earlier volume *Mind & Body Metamorphosis* (ISBN 978-1-84024-549-3) also available from www.mindandbodymetamorphosis.co.uk

"All endings are also beginnings. We just don't know it at the time"

Mitch Albom